AN
AMBIGUOUS
GRIEF

AN AMBIGUOUS GRIEF

A MEMOIR

DOMINIQUE HUNTER

atmosphere press

Now he has departed from this strange world a little ahead of me. That means nothing. The distinction between past, present and future is only a stubbornly persistent illusion.

— Albert Einstein

ONE

Maui, Hawaii

I am sitting on the deck of our condo in a jumble of flora: bougainvillea, hibiscus, bamboo orchids, ginger, plumeria, and, above all, in the bluest of skies, the tousled heads of skinny palm trees swinging gently in the Hawaiian breeze. At home in Oakland we also have palm trees and bougainvillea, orchids, and hibiscus but they all look washed out somehow, almost anemic. Here, it's as if a painter has breathed a new life into the scenery with wide strokes of bold, vibrant, almost glitzy colors: orange and gold, green on green, violet and blue, purple and red. Beyond them are strips of lawn, sand, ocean. There is a taste of salt in the air.

Your father has adopted a crippled old pigeon with a temper. He demands food with an ugly, throaty cry that annoys me no end.

Everything annoys you, Mom!

I don't know about everything, but this pigeon certainly does. To shut him up I give him bits of cheese

and breadcrumbs, but he'd rather have the granola your father throws at him. Your brother worries that the entire flock of pigeons on the island will end up at our feet to peck around for food, messing up the deck with their droppings.

On the walls, a few lizards pop out from behind the drainpipes. In France, at the sea *chez Mamie*, you would spend hours chasing after them to try and pull their tails off and see if they grew back! You never caught any and never found out, *not for real* as you said, if they grew back. They were ugly little reptiles, those lizards, small and fat and yellowish-brown. Here they are so green and bright that they look fake. One of them stands now frozen on the tiles under the table, at your brother's feet.

"Adrian!" I call, "Look at your feet! There is a lizard so beautiful it looks like a toy!"

It's not just a lizard, Mom. It's a gecko! You know nothing?

I know nothing. Still, you have to admit that with the blue eyeliner around its eyes and the red spot on its butt, it looks fake!

It is a green lizard and it has a name: gecko!

"Mama!" your brother calls out, echoing your words in my head, "It's not a toy and it's not just any lizard. It's a gecko. A Gold Dust Day Gecko."

"A what?"

"A Gold Dust Day Gecko."

"A tongue-twister of a name for a gorgeous beast! How did you know?"

"It's on every tourist brochure on the island!"

"Really?"

"Really."

"I know nothing."
You know nothing!

***

I promised myself that I would start writing you here in the sun, in front of the sea, although after the counting began, you liked neither the sun nor the sea. After the counting began, you even fled the light.

Before the counting you loved it all, life in its entirety and you loved it with a force that I see now was like that of a swimmer packing air in his lungs before diving. I wish you had packed more. I mean, twenty-three years of packing air when the waters are deep and wide isn't much when you think about it. Humans can live to be a hundred now. Why couldn't you?

You're still wondering why? You're kidding, right?

No, I am not! I mean, yes, I am kidding. It's so upsetting! But no, of course, I am not wondering why. I know all too well why when I let myself go there. You couldn't live to be a hundred because of the hell in your head. A hell that only your rituals could relieve.

For a while, until the next time. You complained enough about it, remember? Actually, you complained about it constantly. What was I supposed to do?

I complained, yes, although I wouldn't agree it was constant. I imagine that it must have felt that way to you, but it wasn't. Now, so many months later, it would be easy for me to feel guilty about it, but I don't and won't. When it was happening, I couldn't help it. It was a visceral reaction because your rituals were painful to see and hear. They were invasive.

That's mean!

I suppose it is, but it's the truth. I am not writing a version of us, Dylan; I am writing us. The way it was, the way it felt.

The way you felt.

Of course, the way I felt! How could it be otherwise? I can only do this through the prism of my own eyes, of my own memories, of my own sorrow, and it will, therefore, be no doubt slanted, but it will be honest. In turn, you will have to fill in the way it was for you, the way you felt, but candidly and, like me, without sugarcoating anything.

Now, about your rituals. There was the repetitive opening and closing of doors and drawers – three times, two times three when you thought you didn't do it properly, or had rushed through it. When you opened the fridge, you had to touch every single thing in it before taking out what you wanted. You couldn't cross one doorway to the kitchen and had to go around the dining room to enter it through another doorway.

I remember putting twenty, and then forty dollars in cash on one side of the cursed doorway to entice you in, and still you couldn't. It was wrenching to see. When you walked across the living room on your way to your bedroom, you had to touch the wall, the sofa, the armchair, the console, the bookshelves, all the while avoiding stepping on the rugs.

You needed to perform so many rituals throughout the day to bear the day, Dylan! I wish it wasn't so, but it took its toll on me. I found myself demanding that you stop, which, of course, you couldn't, and which, in turn, left me feeling ashamed.

Do we have to remember that now, Mom?

No, we don't. Not now. Now, I will enjoy Maui and its light, its golden sand, its green lizards...

Geckos!

...and the colony of small black birds with yellow beaks and yellow eyes and yellow feet. Like French women, these birds have a great sense of coordination. They also walk like we do, à *petits pas* and very fast, holding their heads high. I like it here; I feel at home.

It's also emotionally safer for me to find my footing in writing you here, far from home. Here in the tropics, in the Hawaiian breeze and the hot softness of the air, I can lift myself up from, and out of, my sorrow to only think of you as the boy who was blessed by the gods.

There are no gods, Mom, you've said so enough yourself!

Well, being blessed by the gods is an expression, and one needs expressions to better capture the meaning of things, the breadth of things, the madness of things and help bring it all home into one's understanding. But no matter the gods. With or without them, you were a player, charming the world around you.

Glenn insisted it was my charm you inherited, but Glenn didn't know me when I was young. He met me in my late twenties, which *is* young, but I am talking when I was younger still, before I came to California. In California, free of the French cultural grip that held me tight in the straight and narrow, I suppose I sprang forth!

Honestly, before California and your dad, I wasn't so charming. I was way too self-conscious and insecure, although one could argue that charm has nothing to do with being secure. You of all people, charm incarnate, you would become insecure. Then again who isn't at fifteen? At twenty? At thirty, and sometimes forever? I suppose life brings a measure of insecurity upon us all to keep us on our toes.

One sure thing though: You were gorgeous the moment you were born, without a crease, a crinkle, a blemish. It took my breath away when, at the hospital, they deposited you at my side after having checked you over.

Newborns are generally not pretty things; let's agree on that. We coo over them, but it's mostly an emotional response to the appearance of life in its nakedness, its purity, its absolute innocence. In a biblical sense, we are observing life before the Fall. Yet, this brand-new human is usually all wrinkled and crunched up like an old person. You weren't, and that is that. In turn, infants grow into babies, and babies aren't necessarily good-looking either...

... Let's agree on that!

Don't mock me! Babies aren't all beautiful, and it's a fact. You were. I remember my mother saying, "It's not normal to be that, to be this ... well, to be so much when so little. It's not for this earth."

An ominous thing to say, don't you think?

Oh, Mom! It was just Mamie getting all excited about her new grandchild! And that didn't last a day! She always loved Adrian best.

Because Adrian was easier to understand. Because he was her first grandchild. Because they had a special bond. Whatever. After you left, she repeated, "Il était trop pour cette terre." He was too much for this earth, to which I retorted that being too much or too little doesn't matter one iota since there never was any other world to live in.

But forgive me; I am straying. Where was I? Ah yes, I was talking about you in youth when your charm was running high and free, when your entire life was up for grabs, when its promises were limitless. Did you see that? Did you see the effect you had on people?

Not on kids my age, not even on the girls if that's what you're thinking of. But I saw it on grownups, and got pretty quickly that I could use it. Like I could say anything and be believed. I got away with a lot...

So you did, insisting proudly that you were the best liar in the whole wide world. I could have pointed out that you came in second after your grandmother, but I kept my mouth shut about that. You also said that no one could ever catch you at it, but I did. In time, I did. I can even pinpoint when.

Your first year in high school. Your first year in high school being, for us all, the threshold of your *fall*. But you could still fool your father! Ah, yes! And you did so until almost the end. Then again, since Day One you held him in the palm of your hand. Don't get me wrong. You had a very real, very special relationship with him that was lovely to see. He was your friend. Is that why you never called him Dad, but Glenn? Glenn this and Glenn that. You'd ring and say, "I want to talk to Glenn" or "Is Glenn home?" Always Glenn. Why?

I don't know. You called him Glenn.

Well, yes, I am his wife. You were his son. Your brother called him Dad.

So what?

Don't be defensive and hear me out. When my own brother and I were children, my parents called each other

Papa and *Maman*. It was probably a generational thing, since every parent around us called each other Mom and Dad. It made sense, I suppose. You say enough times to your kids *go ask Mom* or *go tell Dad,* you end up calling your better self Mom or Dad. Glenn and I never did.

That would have been so totally weird!

Do you remember that since you referred to him as Glenn, your teacher in pre-K thought that he was your brother?

I remember. She just would not get it into her head that I was talking about my dad. She'd say "Dylan, you're talking about your brother now, yes? And I'd say "No, I am talking about my dad." She would smile then like I was being silly, like she knew better. Until the day he picked me up after school, and I shouted, "Glenn!" She got it then.

Well, who could have believed a child would call his dad by his given name?

Again, Mom, why not and so what?

"So what" is that your dad is the only person in the whole world you can call that. Dad. Papa. Father even, which is what your brother calls Glenn now. It represents that unique bond and frankly, I think it's sad you never did.

Whatever. To me, he was Glenn.

Was. You'll never get another chance to call him Dad and that hurts. Come back, Dylan, come back to us and call him Dad. Hell, come back and call him Glenn, call him whatever you like.

TWO

Oakland. Thanksgiving 2014.

It's a cold day under a blue, undiluted sky. All is still outside, and quiet. It's always quiet on *Mercidonnant.*

Mom, you're the only person to ever call it that, which is weird enough, but since you don't celebrate Thanksgiving in France, it's double weird.

All right, I'll give you that. Now, remember how each year on Thanksgiving morning the four of us would drive to North Berkeley, park somewhere on Euclid Avenue and walk all the way up the hill to Creston Road? We'd check out the tiny two-bedroom stucco house with the tiny white picket fence that we rented for seven years. It had a gorgeous view of the bay, a lovely fireplace and a thick, white carpet in the living room. *In the living room.*

The owner, who was also our neighbor, didn't have any kids so he knew nothing of the reality of daily life with children and a cat on a thick, white carpet. Within months we had changed it into a more practical, and very much office-like, anthracite one. The garage, which had already been transformed into a laundry room, became, when you came along, Adrian's bedroom.

You spent the first eight months of your life there. You lifted yourself up for the first time on the office-like carpet, grabbing the glass top of the coffee table with both hands, your face pinched red with the effort. You were seven months old, and never again did you go on all fours.

That summer you had a Polish nanny, twenty-year-old Magdalena of the rolling accent. Remember her?

Of course, I do! I was already five months old, wasn't I?

Don't be clever. Okay. You don't remember her but you saw the pictures I took of you both in the front yard, yes?

Nope. I don't remember that either.

She always sat you there on a blanket and told you stories in Polish!

She did?

Yes, and you were quite attentive.

How about confused?

Very funny! No, honestly, she was truly something Magdalena! She adored you, fussing and cooing all over you like a mother hen! And whatever the weather, she bundled you up tightly with socks stretched all the way to your knees so you wouldn't catch a cold! She was very maternal, Magdalena. Maternal and sensuous. She loved men with muscles on them, "men with bare backs and shoulders burnt by the sun," she told me once, hugging herself with a frisson.

A frisson?

A shiver of excitement. "Here in Berkeley," she explained, "there are plenty of men who *thing*." She meant "think." Never could form that k on her tongue,

12

Magdalena! "They are the students and the professors. They have big heads. (She meant big minds.) But big heads is not sexy to woman, yes? Big heads don't give the pleasure where it counts."

"And where is that, Magdalena?" I asked.

She sighed then, and squeezed her breasts as if entering some erotic fantasy. "Then there are the men on the roofs!"

She talked like that?

She did, and what a treat that was! Like attending some rehearsal for a very sexy play with a Slavic actress. A blonde, blue-eyed Slavic actress.

Who were the men on the roofs?

That's what I asked her. "Who are the men on the roofs, Magdalena?"

"They are the men that work, you know?" she answered, squeezing her breasts again.

"Oh!" I said, "You're talking about builders, roofers!"

"Yes!" Now with her eyes closed, almost moaning. "Ah! These men, they are brown with the sun and they don't wear shirt. They have big muscles and they look at you with eyes that eat!"

I laughed, and she blushed a little before getting sad and serious. "The problem is, they don't thing these men. They have nothing much to say to woman after the giving of pleasure, you know? And so, it's not so good for me in Berkeley, with only professors and builders."

Mom, to you it's interesting but to me, it's kind of boring. I really don't care about the sexual frustrations of a babysitter I remember nothing about.

But I do, and I was curious about her. Immensely curious.

What was so special about her apart from the fact that she had a funny accent and liked men with burnt backs and greasy hands?

She was special because she was the first person I'd ever met who'd been born and raised under Soviet rule behind the Iron Curtain. We were now in 1991, two years after the fall of the Berlin Wall, and she had just arrived from Krakow. Growing up in a world of deceit and paranoia had left her full of absurd preconceptions and extreme suspicion. She was sure, for instance, that banks and post offices kept files on everyone, that telephones were tapped by the government, that listening-devices were hidden in every apartment so as to catch anyone with subversive ideas.

She had also the weirdest beliefs. That birth-control pills turned women into lesbians, for instance. Her Krakow gynecologist had made sure she understood that. Her father, who was a lawyer, had told her terrible things about Jews and black people, about Gypsies.

I got proof of that the day I saw her grab you from the blanket she had laid you on in the front yard of our house and rush you inside. I was just returning from my morning jog and was about to open the gate of the little white picket fence when it happened. She already had her back to me and practically slammed the front door in my face. I had to knock and call her name for her to unlock it! I asked what on earth was going on, and she announced stiffly that there was *a black man outside*.

I had just noticed a PG&E guy exit his van across the street, and it took me a few seconds to register the craziness of her reaction. And so we talked, and she shared the lies she'd been fed in Poland, telling me that racism and anti-Semitism were passed on to children through their mothers' milk.

She actually told you that?

She did.

Woo.

Yes, woo.

Did you tell her that Glenn was Jewish?

I did. She said she already knew it since you were mutilated. That's the word she chose. Not circumcised, but *mutilated!* When I told her that in the U.S. the practice was blessed by the medical establishment and so widespread - whatever the religion - that over sixty-five percent of all newborn males were circumcised, she was flabbergasted.

And what happened to this Little Miss Ignoramus?

A few months later, we left Berkeley for Oakland, leaving her behind. We said goodbye and promised we would keep in touch, but we never did. About a year later, I bumped into her on the street in Berkeley. After many hugs and kisses, she told me that she had at long last decided upon the right kind of man for her.

"No man on the roof?" I teased.

She leaned closer and whispered forcefully, "*Nie,* no man on the roofs, and no professors! I now go to Alameda to find for myself a real man."

"In Alameda? A real man?"

"Yes. A soldier. On army base!"

"I guess I would have never been a real man then! No way I could have ever joined the army!"

That's for sure! For one thing, you hated physical activities! You even hated walking! Not to mention waking up early.

And war! I would have hated war. I mean, and risk dying?

Oh no, you would never risk that. Not you.

Mom!

Sorry.

***

Each year on Thanksgiving morning, the four of us would also walk through Glenn's old neighborhood in the same Berkeley hills. We'd walk and he'd point out at the houses of his primary school friends, remembering them, telling us stories. One such morning, as we stood in front of the house he grew up in, he told us how, every time he came back from a visit to the orthodontist, his father would rearrange his braces! It's no wonder his teeth are crooked!

His father wanted to become a dentist, yes?

Yes, but he couldn't, so he studied chemistry instead.

What do you mean he couldn't?

Since the 1930s, most medical schools in the U.S. - most specifically private colleges such as Cornell, Harvard, Yale, had very rigid quotas on the number of Jews admitted. At Yale, for instance, the regulations were quite clear: "Never admit more than five Jews, take only two Italian Catholics, and take no blacks at all. This until the early 1960s! This here, in the U.S., the country of immigrants, the country of the Statue of Liberty, the country whose soldiers from the 6th Armored Division entered, in April 1945, the concentration camp of Buchenwald.

Jesus!

No, not Jesus. Jesus was nowhere in sight. But enough of this. Let's go back to the Berkeley hills on Thanksgiving mornings where we walked and talked and laughed and argued about nothing and everything.

And where you always got pissed off about something one of us said! That sent you walking away from us, way ahead of us. Glenn would roll his eyes and say it's okay; she is French.

I'd give anything to get upset once more and walk away from you. I'd give anything for Glenn to roll his eyes and say again, *it's okay; she is French!*

Today, we didn't go back and neither of us said a word about it. Then again, we didn't go last year either. We knew that going without you was impossible. Instead, Glenn and I went for a long walk in the neighborhood, and your brother took a sixty-mile bike ride.

Adrian is a sport nut!

And always was. Doesn't take after me, that's for sure. You did. Sports left you entirely cold, in that very French way of shrugging it off as if it was an absolute absurdity, the ultimate eccentricity of those who enjoy sweating, grown men running after a ball, grown men wanting to show off. Show off what? Their muscles? Their stamina? Their health? No one ever said, but being French, we knew.

You had a taste of it in high school, though, and you could have become hooked. Of that, I have no doubt. Like me, you were always the all or nothing kind of personality, and having no real choice of middle ground in sports, it would have been all. As a result, you could have put your restlessness and obsessive thinking into it. You *would* have if they had not decided to punish you for your behavior by first throwing you off the football team...

Where I was already killing it!

...Where you were already killing it. What a waste! More waste the following spring with track and field. Off the team again by way of punition! But that's altogether another nightmare. A nightmare for later since just mentioning it distresses me.

And pisses me off.

We'll go there when get there. When we can no longer avoid it.

I don't want to go there. Never ever. It's too humiliating.

But it happened, Dylan, and it's a crucial part of your history when your history took the saddest turn of all the saddest turns in anyone's history. It felt like blood.

Blood? Mom, I am so rolling my eyes right now!

Roll all you want. It felt like blood when they got us to sit like two condemned prisoners in a room like a courtroom, with all your teachers sitting in a row across the table, their faces hard as stones, to tell me how uncontrollable you were, and how I might want to consider having you locked up. One of them said precisely that, remember?

My art teacher, of all people! And that was my best class! I knew it killed him to have to give me an A. But since everybody saw how good I was and commented on it, what could he do, huh?

Not give you an A+.

That's right, he never did.

You were no angel, Dylan, and I was certainly not excusing your behavior in the classroom. You were unruly and disruptive, but you were no delinquent. You were a sixteen-year-old kid struggling with the learning process, a fact that they, the educators, heartlessly ignored. That's what got to me. Their judgment of you and me without a shred of empathy. I am sure this wasn't helped by the fact that you were a social animal, and a popular one at that. Not to mention that when caught acting out or lying, you got cocky and pig-headed. You had a big, big mouth, Dylan!

Hmmm! I wonder where I got it from!

I'll own up to that one. Still, you don't treat a kid with behavioral problems like a criminal. Behavioral problems don't fall from the sky. They are rooted in insecurities, and in your case, academic insecurities. You don't insult such a kid in front of his mother, you don't keep hurling accusations at them both with no offer whatsoever of remedial help, and you don't dismiss them in such a haughty manner.

It got so bad I had to excuse myself and leave the room for a few minutes, to go stand in the corridor and cry.

Mom, enough already! You said it's a story for later, you said we'll talk about it when we get there, and you've kept ranting about it ever since. I hate it.

Okay. Okay. I'll stop.

Let's take a break, please?

Let's.

***

Dylan, are you there?

Of course, I am. Where would I go?

I am sorry I got carried away.

Seriously!

Meanwhile, it's still Thanksgiving and I am cooking.

Let me guess, no turkey?

I really don't like that bird. Not to mention that it's one of the ugliest beasts on earth. I don't eat ugly things. Would you eat a toad? A bat? A vulture?

Gee, don't you eat frogs in France? And snails?

Frogs aren't toads, and we just eat their legs. You wouldn't know they were frogs if you weren't told.

Right. You'd think they were giant grasshoppers' legs!

That's a thought! Actually, I never liked frog legs. They are tasteless. As for snails, they are cute and...

...Slobbering!

And as tasteless as frog legs! It's all about the sauce. Tomato sauce, garlic sauce, pesto...

...Mom? Where are you going with this?

To the duck I am braising, and will serve with...

Stop! I don't want to hear. I really don't.

I suppose not, since you won't be able to eat it. You always loved food and you were in such a hurry to get to it that you rejected my breasts at three months old. Honestly, I didn't mind since you went at them as if you wanted to yank them off my chest! You rejected my breasts and went straight to solid food. There isn't a picture of your early years in which you aren't holding a piece of bread or a piece of cheese or an ice cream. You loved everything! You even loved spinach!

You tried everything with no qualms nor hesitation, as if you knew you wouldn't have time to taste it all.

THREE

I tortured myself a long time trying to figure out how to go about writing you. I first thought of a tale, something *à la* Boris Vian in *l'Ecume des Jours* where he turned his beloved Chloé's illness into a lily that grew inside her lungs. Because of the repetitiveness of your rituals, I imagined a hamster running endlessly inside a ball in your bedroom. As Chloé's cancer grew, Vian had the walls of their apartment shrink around them. I would have the hamster grow and grow until it filled the ball, and then the entire room. It would, in turn, take you over and become you, just as Boo did.

That's weird and disturbing! It reminds me of that book I had to read in middle school about a guy who wakes up changed into this ugly giant insect.

A monstrous vermin, in the text. That's *The Metamorphosis*, a sixth-grade summer assignment that Glenn read to you because reading was always stressful for you.

I liked that story a lot.

Because it was disturbing?

Yeah. And a bit creepy.

I thought the choice of Kafka a bit much for seventh

grade, but that was the French Academy, and the French Academy always pushed the envelope when it came to its curriculum.

In any case, the hamster metaphor being rather limiting, I dropped the idea.

Limiting?

The more I thought about it, the more I realized that I could not take it very far. It would be more appropriate for a short story or a play. A play *à la* Ionesco.

À la what?

Ionesco. A great French avant garde playwright. Well, not entirely French since he was...

I don't care what he was, Mom!

Fine. Great writer, though. You'd have loved his sense of the absurd. He ridiculed everything and...

Blah blah blah...

Okay, let's just say that I dropped the idea of a monstrous hamster to consider writing a straight record of what happened, of who you were before the onset of the disorder, and of what became of you after, as the disorder grew.

But that didn't feel quite right either. It was too clinical, I thought, and you deserved better. You deserved a story. So, upon returning from Maui, I went back to the few paragraphs I had written, determined to expand on them, while keeping you alongside me for the ride. After all, you had appeared with the intention of staying, right?

Appeared?

Well, yes. Over my shoulder. In my head. In my ear to be sure since you commented on something. What was it? Ah, yes, first about the fact that everything irritates me, which, I'll admit, is not untrue, and then about how I *constantly* complained about your rituals, which, you'll admit, isn't quite true.

I'll admit nothing.

See? That's precisely what I mean by keeping you alongside me. We are having a conversation, and a conversation is the perfect way of writing you. You'll be able to comment, to explain, to calibrate or recalibrate, and I'll be able to push your buttons without real consequences. Together, we'll come to better understand the you who failed you.

Whatever.

***

It's now Friday evening, November 27th, the day after Thanksgiving. Your grandmother will be arriving tomorrow to spend the winter with us, as she has every year since papi left us. What with Manouche who looks like she put ten years on her hips over the summer, poor thing, we will now have two old and smelly ladies in our midst.

Manouche will keep chewing at her paws, and Mamie will keep repeating herself - how she can't believe she is here in America, how if she had been told when she was a girl in France in the Thirties that one day she would travel to America! That her daughter - *her daughter!* - would marry an American! Not that any French men would have ever wanted to marry me, what with my personality.

"Actually, no. Not your personality," she'll correct herself. "Your personality is good enough; I'll give you that. But your temper! *Ooh la la!* How could a French man deal with your temper? Well, that's easy enough to answer: He could not. Now, how you managed to hook an American, for the life of me I couldn't say, but how nice."

She had seen Americans before. First in the summer of 1945, at *la libération* in Paris, and how beautiful they all were, these soldiers with their white, even teeth! They chewed gum and had big smiles. *Des sourires pleins de dents!* Smiles full of teeth. And they were all so young, they looked like children! *Ils étaient tous si jeunes, on aurait dit des enfants!*

Today, your grandmother has forgotten all about the American soldiers of the summer of 1945, but she is in America where her daughter always wanted to be, in California of all places, and how wonderful is that for someone who began her life so poorly. She will remind me and herself yet again how she started her life as an abandoned child in an orphanage, and is now ending it splendidly as an old woman with family on both sides of the world.

Surely it is better this way than the other way around, because if you were lucky enough to have had a golden childhood in a loving family, no adult life could possibly ever satisfy you, not ever completely - on either side of the world. In other words, she herself was lucky to have been unlucky at birth since now, at her grand age, she was in America.

"Better still," she told me last year, "I am in California and do you know how people feel when you tell them you are going to spend the winter at your daughter's in California? In San Francisco?"

"Maman," I said, "we live in Oakland."

"Yes," she scoffed, "but nobody knows about Oakland in France. Oakland brings nothing to the French mind, while San Francisco - Ah, San Francisco! A magic place, that's what it brings to the French mind, and people feel envious, jealous even, when you tell them you are going there."

And she was quite, quite satisfied with that.

She will repeat it all again, word for word, and then go on and on telling me stories and tall tales that will drive me mad, since I won't be able to believe a word she says and no wonder *you*, Dylan, had an imagination! It skipped a generation to land squarely on your shoulders.

Mom, I get my imagination from you. You are the one writing stories.

Perhaps, but your grandmother was the first grand lady of the *rewrite*. She rewrote her own life so many times, there were so many different versions over the years that to this day I can barely find my way through them. But through them she took me, always earnestly, always insisting that *that* version was the true one, *Que Dieu me punisse si je mens!* May God strike me if I lie.

One thing I've learned about God: He doesn't strike fanciful ladies.

You have nothing to worry about then!

Dylan! I might be a bit imaginative, but I am not fanciful. However, as I said, your grandmother reinvented her childhood time and time again. But you already know about that.

Not really. Just that she was an orphan. If you told me more, I probably forgot about it the moment you stopped talking!

How nice of you to say that.

Come on, Mom, I was a kid, more interested in TV shows and video games than I was about my grandmother's life story.

But you loved stories!

Then, obviously, you didn't tell me any! Or you did it badly. Or I forgot. Now would be a good time.

I don't know, Dylan. I am not writing about my mother.

You always said that family history is important to know if we want to understand who we are.

Yes. Because among other things, we are the recipients of our ancestry. Vastly diluted, no doubt, probably disjointed and distorted - who knows? - but a recipient nevertheless.

And I want to understand who I was, so Mamie is a good place to start.

I suppose. I'll try to keep it short.

In the first version of her birth that she gave me when I was a girl, she was found on the doorstep of a church, carefully bundled up and with gold coins inside her blanket. The priest took her straight to the Dominican nuns.

And kept the coins?

Very funny, Dylan. No, the priest didn't keep the coins because there weren't any coins, and your grandmother wasn't found bundled up on the doorstep of a church. Which is too bad since, as a child, I loved that version. It was rather romantic, don't you think?

More like sad.

I suppose. In any case, in the next version, her father

was a pilot in the army, and her mother, Odelia Roynel, was a nurse. That much is true since it's written on her birth certificate: Mother: Odelia Roynel. Profession: *infirmière*. Father: *inconnu* or unknown. They'd met in north Africa on a French military base, and she'd become pregnant.

He'd brought her back home to France to his very *bourgeois* family who didn't approve of her since she was a nobody. They threatened to cut off his inheritance if he insisted on marrying her, and since he was a gentleman in name only, he gave her up. They kept Odelia as part of their household staff until the birth of her baby. When your grandmother was born, they took her to the nuns and threw Odelia out. Cruel, yes?

And super mean.

And not true. In a more realistic rewrite, perhaps even the true one, Odelia had an affair with one of the doctors she worked with and became pregnant. The good doctor, who was probably married, wanted nothing to do with the baby. Odelia had no choice but to bring her infant daughter to the nuns. What else could she do? In the 1920s, an unmarried mother was an instant outcast. She would have lost her job and ended up in the streets, like Fantine in *Les Misérables,* but without Jean Valjean to come and rescue her.

Jean who? What are you talking about, Mom?

I am talking about *Les Misérables,* one of the great French novels of all time. A dozen films were made of it, and a musical on Broadway, and, as if that wasn't enough, a movie of the musical.

So?

So, in the book, ex-convict Jean Valjean rescues

Fantine, a young woman who has to prostitute herself to pay for her daughter's care. We are in the 1830s, and life in the streets is quite sordid. A century later an unmarried mother wasn't better off, so I assume that not wanting to end up like Fantine, your great-grandmother brought her daughter to the Dominican nuns.

Mamie was always tortured about that. Had she been rescued? Or abandoned? Did her mother really have no choice but to get rid of her? She could never be sure, could she? And it haunted her. I can understand that. And I can understand why, as a little girl starved for affection, she imagined a different reality, many different realities.

She carried them all into adulthood. Once, she told me that Odelia had actually kept her for a few years. That she remembered clearly a beautiful woman bending over her bed, smiling at her, and telling a man - tall, he was very tall, she insisted - "Look how beautiful my petite Colette is!"

I write down this fantasy of hers, and I find it difficult to bear.

What a fucking story, Mom! I can...

Stop it with the F word!

...tell you that if I had heard it before, even as a kid, no way I would have forgotten it. How come you never wrote about it?

How do you know I didn't?

Because if you had, I would have read it. Not that I would have had a choice!

Meaning?

Meaning that each time you wrote a story, I had to read it. So did Adrian. We loved your stories, I swear; it's just that you always insisted we read them right this minute even if we were busy doing other things, or we didn't feel like reading them right that fucking minute. I even...

Stop swearing. How many times do I have to ask?

...promised you that I would one day turn them into movies, remember?

I do, and never doubted it. You were always so very clever with your camera! We gave you your first one...

For my ninth birthday. I remember.

You shot little movies in the kitchen with characters made out of wire, string, and foil. Ketchup for blood, charcoal for eyes. No mouth. "No mouth?" I asked. "I am making silent movies!" you replied, rolling your eyes.

You could have become a great director. No, you *would have* become a great director. I was secretly so sure that one day you would get an Oscar, that Glenn and I would be sitting in the Dolby Theater in Los Angeles cheering you, tears rolling down my face. If you hadn't gotten sick.

I didn't "get" sick, Mom. As you kept telling me, I came that way. Probably the distorted part of my ancestry?

Dylan...

...and over the years one fucked up thing after another caught up with me. As in dyslexia, first.

Dyslexia is too large a word. Let's say that you had a learning disorder, *and,* yes, that's where it began. Halfway through second grade, we were told that you weren't up to speed with deciphering words. Then again, lots of kids aren't to speed to begin with. Kids grow teeth at different times. Kids grow in height and speed at different times. What's the difference? None, we thought. So, we waited a bit.

And still, I didn't get up to speed.

You learned differently, that's what! But since you were in a school that taught only a certain way - the French way - it was a bit of a struggle. In the fourth grade, you were evaluated at UC Berkeley and had to endure hours of testing ...

Endure? You're kidding me? It always happened during school days and everyone there was super nice. I loved it!

That's when we found out, without surprise, that your right brain, which is the seat of creativity, was dominant. That you weren't wired to use logic, to form strategies, to...

Blah blah blah.

There is nothing blah blah blah about this, Dylan. This is science. Your left brain, which uses linear logic and rationality, and which, sadly, is at the base of all academic and social systems in the western world - your left brain was defective. You couldn't conform, and therefore, you couldn't fit. Since you couldn't fit, you were downgraded and punished.

Whatever.

Your dad and I didn't do "whatever." Your dad and I tried very hard to understand the how and why. That's why you were tested again in the fifth grade. This time, you were diagnosed with dyscalculia.

Stop it with the big words! Say it as it was: I sucked at math. I sucked at math and at reading and at writing and, as if that wasn't enough, it turned out I also had ADHD.

Which is perhaps a side effect of a suppressed creative mind? Of a mind who processes information differently? To be sure, ADHD goes rather well with dyslexia. So why keep them apart, huh?

Not funny.

Sorry.

Final fuck and biggest of all: OCD, which, in turn, gave me anxieties and panic attacks.

OCD might also be a side effect of...

Dyslexia?

Of your need to fly. I am simplifying, of course, but...

Who the hell cares since, according to you, it was all but inevitable? Since I came that way? Since my bloodline is all about suppressed creativity?

Don't you ridicule me, Dylan Hunter! And, no, we most certainly don't...

...come from nowhere. I know. You've said it a zillion times: Every basic thing we are made of is genetic, like eye color, like the size of your butt, the shape of your nose...

Stop mimicking my voice!

...like weak stomachs and bad teeth, like the color of the skin and the slamming of doors, like the tendency to lie and rearrange reality. Me getting that last two from Mamie, and dyslexia from your brother, yes?

And Mamie before him. She always had a hard time spelling and reading, your grandmother.

Yeah. And one of Papi's sisters had OCD, right? Way back then?

Way back into the twentieth century, yes, when it wasn't called OCD yet. As a matter of fact, I don't remember ever hearing a medical word, or any word at all except "peculiar," to explain my aunt, who by the way was also my godmother. To be sure, it was no longer thought the devil had entered the soul of those suffering from the disorder, and no exorcist was called to beat him out of her body.

Woo! Really, they did that? Like in the movie The Exorcist?

Something like that. But that was in much older times. From the 1800s on, it was recognized as a mental illness, and, in turn, called monomania, impulsive insanity, disease of the emotions due to defective heredity...

As you said, ancestry! They had something there.

The term obsessive-compulsive disorder wasn't coined until quite recently.

Okay, Mom. Who cares when it was coined? How about your godmother?

My tall, dark, languid and penny-pinching godmother, who never gave me more than a couple of French francs at Christmas, and never acknowledged my birthday?

Because it's the day after Christmas?

Yes. I assume that the couple of francs were meant for both. One franc for my birthday, one franc for Christmas. In her defense, she seemed out of place in the world. Resigned to whatever it was that underwhelmed her. As for her peculiarities, as Mamie so delicately put it, she had many, like a need to constantly reposition her spoon, her knife, her fork, and her wine glass at the dinner table; to readjust her napkin on her lap; to turn the ring on her finger this way and that. My brother and I used to count how many times she'd do it throughout a meal. We'd even bet candies on it.

You bet candies on her OCD?! That's messed up, Mom!

No, not really. We were children, and children notice oddities. Since no grownup ever talks about them, since they're like a big dirty secret, children deal with them by making fun of them. Children also tend to mock people when they don't know what to make of them. My godmother was definitely one of those.

You also said that you and Mamie tend to count?

We do. We count when we walk upstairs, when we buy apples and potatoes and whatever else that can be counted, when we clip flowers in her garden – one flower, two flowers, three flowers, when we drink water from a bottle - one gulp, two gulps, three gulps — like that. And let's not forget that I suffer from Misophonia.

From what?

From an extreme sensitivity to sounds. Someone slurping their coffee or chewing loudly can drive me out of a room and into a state of intense gripe! Someone humming or whistling, or worse, chatting into their mobile for all to hear, can make me leave a queue in a store, and then the store, the neighborhood, the city, the country, the continent, the planet, carrying within me unspeakable murderous thoughts! Oh, how I would torture the offender!

By lecturing him to death?

Possibly.

You absolutely would, Mom!

In any case, as you see, I am not all that neurologically sound either.

I remember you being obsessed with us chewing with

our mouths closed.

Yes! To a point where once, while having dinner at a friend's house, your brother, then six years old, asked his friend to close his mouth while eating! The mother later called me to apologize for her son's poor table manners! And poor manners that was, but reacting to them had nothing to do with Misophonia.

Weird name.

For a weird disorder that was not scientifically acknowledged until recently. I used to feel so bloody guilty for being so easily and profoundly annoyed by so many sounds. I thought it was behavioral. I thought it was my fault, that I was too uptight.

Too French?

Very funny, Dylan Hunter! But as we both know, it's never that simple. We probably all have some neurological twist that people judge neurotic.

And, to add to the list, Glenn's side of the family had a history of depression?

His mom had some serious compulsions. She would get up at night to bake pies that could have fed the entire neighborhood. She also did strange things with her daughters' clothes. After she died, they found in a closet all the garments that had mysteriously disappeared over the years.

The sweaters, the skirts, pants, and shirts were all there but unstitched, the hems undone, all the buttons, zippers, and pockets removed. The mangled clothes were left in a bag while the buttons, sleeves, pockets, and zippers were carefully arranged on a shelf. A pile of zippers, a pile of buttons, a pile of pockets, a pile of sleeves.

That's messed up!

It's sad. That's what it is. Like something ignored or forgotten, something abandoned, disowned. It's a statement of utter surrender.

To what?

Hopelessness.

She must have felt so lonely.

Yes.

And one of Glenn's sisters hasn't left her house in years?

Practically. She is agoraphobic.

And the other was a heroin addict?

She was when she was young. When their mom died, a friend gave her some heroin to help her feel better, and she got hooked. It's a long and painful story. Now, she is addicted to Jesus, which, given the alternative, is a good thing.

Gee Mom, what were my chances?

Your brother didn't get any of it.

Lucky him.

That's genetic roulette for you.

So unfair!

You can say that again. But I believe that one day science will be able to correct that unfairness. One day, science will fix OCD and dyslexia and ADHD and all the rest of mental illnesses. It will rewire whatever it is that's malfunctioning or replace what's missing. I believe that the human brain is similar to a huge computer whose software, so far, has been impossible to fully decrypt. But I don't doubt that we will. We will, but meanwhile, we can't heal people like you, and it's heartbreaking.

FOUR

You were eighteen months old. I had just pulled you out of the car seat in the parking lot of our supermarket in Berkeley. Your feet barely on the ground, you bolted out toward the doors. I caught you right in front of an elderly couple standing at the entrance, waiting for a taxi. As I lifted you into my arms the lady said, "What a beautiful child!" She was tall and dignified, with piercing gray eyes.

"That he is," I replied. "A handful, too!"

"I can see him surrounded by crowds," she added eerily. "People are cheering."

"Excuse me?"

"My wife has the gift of precognition," the old man said gently. "Not with everybody, mind you, but when she does it's very vivid. Like a vision, you know. She sees."

Then their taxi pulled in and they left me standing there with you wriggling in my arms, wondering.

Later, every time you got into trouble I thought of that encounter. I thought of the piercing gray eyes, of the dignified ease with which she told me of her vision, and I made myself believe that you would be all right. People would cheer you; you would be loved and celebrated, perhaps as a great movie director, perhaps as a great politician, what with your way of charming the world around you. I must say, though, that in my books, becoming a movie director would have been more honorable than becoming a politician.

You can close your book. I am not going to be anything.

***

Oakland, December 1st

Your eighty-nine-year-old grandmother arrived three days ago, after traveling some sixteen hours. She got up at four a.m. to drive forty-five minutes to the Montpellier airport where she took the ninety-minute flight to Paris. There she waited a couple of hours at Charles de Gaulle for her flight to the U.S. She then flew ten-and-a-half hours to San Francisco, where she landed as fresh as spring time, to be picked up by your brother.

Safely delivered at home mid-afternoon, she asked for a glass of whiskey orange, no ice please. I fed her some goat cheese on toast by the blazing fire Glenn had made.

"This American goat cheese is absolutely delicious," she announced after a bite, before scoffing, "And to think that *we* think *we* are the kings of cheese making!"

"We are, Maman, we still are," I said calmly. "The one you are eating is French."

"It is?" she asked dubiously. When you lie your way

through life about pretty much everything, you tend to think that everyone else does the same.

It took her another three hours to decide that she was tired.

"I'll go to bed now if you don't mind," she said.

She slept over seventeen hours straight.

She hasn't changed. "At my age," she concedes, "one is fossilized."

She does look very much ancient with her bad teeth — she lost two, another is shaky, and she still won't brush them daily.

Mom, she won't brush them, like, ever!

Let's not remind ourselves of that. As I was saying, she looks ancient and very old world. No old lady looks quite like that in the Bay Area.

To begin with, they all have teeth!

Gleaming white and aligned. And mostly false.

False?

As in prosthesis. I wonder, though, are these old ladies of the gleaming teeth otherwise healthy? Your eighty-nine-year old grandmother hasn't any pain anywhere. She takes no meds and complains of nothing. She hasn't seen a doctor in years. That's a comfort.

However, she did find Manouche aged, which is true. Manouche suffered greatly from allergies this year. She had a rash all over her back, and she lost the little shepherd skirt on her behind, which now looks like it was shaved. Your grandmother stared at it curiously for a moment, then asked what happened. I told her that Manouche, too, was getting old, and she remarked that, *Dieu merci,* her own ass hadn't gone the same way.

So Mamie!

Ah, yes! She has no filter whatsoever when it comes to saying things the way she sees or thinks them.

You are just like her.

About speaking my mind, yes. But I do I have some filters.

Some.

Dylan! In any case, we spent yesterday afternoon looking at the photo albums I made of our lives. The first ten years with you were a triumph, Dylan, and we loved revisiting them picture by picture, story after story. You truly were something! Always grinning, grimacing, or mimicking, and with a smile so spirited and knowing that who would have thought anything bad could ever happen to you? And when you laughed, it was with such might it hurts to know no one will ever hear it again. Had you stayed with us and grown healthy, your laughter would have lifted mountains and parted the seas.

"Look!" Mamie said, pointing. "He did laugh his way through childhood!"

"Except when he didn't get his way," I reminded her, and we both sighed deeply.

The legend in the family is that your very first word wasn't Mom, wasn't even Glenn - although, to be sure, Glenn was a close contender. Your very first word was *mine,* and the legend might as well be true. Were you giving us advance notice of your future compulsions? Of the obsessive thoughts that would come to plague you? I believe you were.

The fact is that we couldn't take you to a sand box where other children were playing without you grabbing every toy in sight and claiming it as yours. *"Mine!"* You'd howl when we tried to pry a toy away from you, *"Mine!"* And you'd hold on to each one for dear life until, exhausted, your hands gave up. You would turn them into fists then, so furious and frustrated were you at having lost the battle!

Soon enough, we'd show up at a playground and the other mothers would gather their children and leave. We would change playgrounds. We went to all the playgrounds in town and then to all the playgrounds in the next town, and the next and pretty soon to all the playgrounds in the state, in the country, and then to all the playgrounds in the whole wide world.

And all the other worlds.

And all the other worlds.

We always came home exhausted.

To this day, Mamie remembers the time you jumped into the big red pedal car of a young Japanese boy who had just climbed out of it. You gripped the wheel with such force it took four adults to pull you up and out. Two Japanese parents and two French grandparents unable to communicate with one another.

Or the day you grabbed the camera a proud young dad had carefully placed on a picnic table. Your fingers clutched the leather strap, and you simply would not let go of it. In the end, the man had to detach the strap from the camera to recover it unharmed. You, of course, instantly threw the strap away and got straight back at the camera - once more, carefully deposited on the picnic table - before anyone could blink an eye.

What happened next?

What do you think?

Did I break it?

I don't know. Mamie screamed, and that must have shocked you into dropping it because that's what you did. You dropped the camera and before the man could react, Papi threw you over his shoulder, and you all fled the park.

Really? You're sure Mamie was not exaggerating?

I am sure, because Papi confirmed it.

Okay. Let's say I broke the thing. I was, what? Two, three years old? Don't tell me I was the only kid who ever did things like that.

Of course, you weren't the only kid who did such things, except that there was something about the way you went at it, the way you held on to whatever you had claimed, that was - I don't know, urgent? Urgent and fierce?

I was already the compulsive brat, that's what!

Really, Dylan, have you ever heard of a three-year-old guest at a friend's fifth birthday party who leaves the kitchen where everyone is having lunch - why have lunch like everyone else? - to go into the living room where all the birthday boy's presents are gathered and starts opening them, crying out loud that they aren't what *he* wanted?

That's pretty funny!

It was less funny for the birthday boy, I can tell you that, although I didn't hear about it until years later. His mother had asked Adrian, who was also at the party, not to say a word to me. Then again, she is a great friend and she was fond of you. She saw no malice in your action. Same thing when you grabbed their front doorknob and wouldn't let go, holding on till doomsday, your face as red as a tomato, your fingers white as chalk, wanting to get in at all cost because you loved it so much there.

"Mon Dieu" Mamie cried out, "How many candles did he have on this birthday cake?"

She was pointing a finger at a picture taken on your third birthday. You were bent over the cake, your cheeks all puffed up, ready to blow the life out of them. Except that there were not only three candles, but ten. You had refused to blow only three, *just because*. Same thing the year before when you had refused to blow only two, and the following year when you would refuse to blow only four. You must have blown dozens of birthday candles!

Were you trying to blow out all the candles of all the birthdays you would never have?

And at the ice cream parlor, was it the same unconscious knowing that propelled you, in less time than it takes to say it, to grab the ice cream cups left unattended on the surrounding tables? Where you trying to eat all the ice cream you could for all the years you wouldn't live?

Remembering, I sighed again.

"He was as stubborn as a mule," Mamie said, pointing at another picture of the cake with too many candles.

Honestly, if you hadn't been so extraordinarily tender, living with you would have been a nightmare! Mamie was right; you were stubborn as a mule, not to mention mercurial and temperamental, but also sweet and caring. In other words, a mass of contradictions.

"And a beautiful liar," Mamie went on, still perusing the photo album. "No wonder he got away with so much!"

To your credit, you never held a grudge when reprimanded or chastised. You always bounced back with laughter and apologies.

I was good at apologizing.

Hmm! Could it just have been another clever deception?

I am not saying.

***

As for the "mine" stories, I see now that yes, they were ominous, presaging what would happen at puberty. Of course, not every child who howls *mine!* and holds on to things with such ferocity later develops OCD and a whole set of anxieties. But how about saying that a teen who does develop anxieties and/or OCD was probably showing some sort of intense disposition as a kid?

Does it matter?

It does to me.

And then what? Let's say that yes, I showed signs of a future disorder in a very innocent way and that you were made aware of it, what could have you done?

Not a whole lot, I suppose, but perhaps some? Perhaps enough? Like thinking it through? Like taking you out of the French school system? Like moving away from Oakland? Like making sure you got hooked early on something healthy and addictive like a sport of endurance? I don't know, Dylan! I am just exploring possibilities.

Whatever, Mom. I don't care anymore.

You should. You deserve it. You were quite unique. Then again, being your mother, I might be biased.

Might be?

Biased but aware. Aware and inquisitive. Inquisitive and driven. Driven to dig into the mystery of you, of your mind, of what it was that damaged it.

Meanwhile, your grandmother said something quite insightful. She remarked that no one could ever really get mad at you since none of your actions, like the grabbing of toys in sand boxes or other people's ice cream cups at ice-cream parlors were done in a mean or duplicitous way. You were truly and wholeheartedly convinced that everything in the world was yours.

I believe that just as we all carry within ourselves our destiny, you carried within yourself the knowledge that your life would be cut short, and that you had to grab it all while you could.

FIVE

In bed at night, as sleep eludes me, I often have a song circling in my head, one of the French yeah!yeah! songs from my youth that seems to come out of nowhere. It must have tucked itself so deeply into my psyche that it only pops out in the vacuum left by my insomnia.

It wouldn't be unpleasant if the song wasn't running on a loop and if I was able to stop it. But no matter what I do, it keeps going. I try to pry my mind off it by focusing on something else, something tangible and dear to me, like what new plants I will get in the spring for the garden or our trip to France in the summer - shall it be in the Dordogne or Provence? Shall we skip Paris? I think about the book I am reading or about the meal I will cook on Sunday for your brother who comes every Sunday to be with us since you left.

I think about everything I can think of, but the damn song remains in the background like a soundtrack to my thoughts, and it drives me crazy.

I think of you, then. I think of how your own obsessive thoughts seared your mind with the fear that Glenn or I could die, that one of us had cancer and was hiding it, and the anxiety that followed was so powerful you had to perform your rituals. At home by closing and opening doors, taking a few steps this way and that, going outside to tap-tap-tap on the wall with two knuckles, rhythmically and with a pattern: Three knocks and stop, three knocks and stop, then five knocks and stop. Again. Three knocks and stop, three knocks and stop, then five knocks and stop. If ever a third knuckle touched the wall, you had to start all over. Three knocks and stop, three knocks and stop, and then five knocks. At school by tapping quietly under your desk with the rubber end of a pencil - tap-tap-tap, tap-tap-tap, tap-tap-tap.

I see now how absolutely mad it was, like being unable to turn off a faucet all the way, and being forever condemned to hear the drip, drip, drip of water inside the pipes of your brain.

No wonder you needed drugs. No wonder you went out and found them! Who could blame you?

You did! Glenn did! Adrian did! You all did!

Of course, we did. You were our son! You were his brother! It was so very raw and personal and complicated, don't you see? How could we allow ourselves to agree to your choice of relief, which was a complete shutdown of your mind? It was maddening, and there were so little choices. Cigarettes? I fought Glenn to let you smoke...

Outside the house, off our property, out on the street!

...thinking it was a minor health scare compared to the alternative. And yes, outside on the street. Of course, outside on the street! Not that it helped any.

It helped me stop chewing my fingernails for a while,

but that wasn't enough. Nothing was enough. Not even the weed Glenn gave me.

You called it hippie weed because it was so mild. Meanwhile, what you smoked didn't just get you high, it got you wasted.

That was the idea, Mom.

And you went right back to chewing your fingernails, down to the quick.

You called me chewy! Chewy or stumpy!

You called me wrinkly!

Only fair.

Let's high five that!

***

Yesterday, we had another mass shooting in America. The year isn't even over and there already have been more of them than the number of days, if you'll believe it!

I believe it. Papi always said that Americans are still a bunch of cowboys shooting their way through life!

Yes, my dad was of that opinion. Then again, he was also of the opinion that the Italians are thieves, the Germans too hegemonic ...

Hege-- what?

Dominant. The Germans are way too dominant, and, what with their bull fights and their primitive Catholicism, the Spaniards are, to put it politely, coarse. As for the English, well, to begin with they know nothing about food, they drive on the wrong side of the road, they use feet and stones for measurement, and to top it all, they killed Joan of Arc! If you pointed out that we'd actually sold her to them at a high price so she'd be put on trial and burnt at the stake, he shrugged it off as if it was a mere footnote in the annals of our glorious history! In any case, about the mass shooting yesterday, we have now more innocent people dead.

What happened?

A student shot his classmates. Since Columbine it's been a regular occurrence. And when it's not a student shooting students, it's cops shooting black men in the back, or an angry man killing co-workers. We are such a fractured and violent society! I am thinking, will it ever stop? I am thinking, where is the world going?

For me, it's going nowhere, Mom!

Please don't say that, it totally breaks me. Just stand here at my shoulder every time I sit down to write you. I am going somewhere, and I am going there with you. Deal?

... ...

I'll take that as a yes. Where were we?

With mass killing. Let's drop it, please?

Yes. Let's drop it and return to your boyhood.

When my life was still happening.

When you were sweet and carefree, funny as hell, and a real pain.

How could I be all of those at once?

I don't know, Dylan, but it certainly summarizes the boy you were! The stubbornness, the single-mindedness, the charm. We could call it the Dylan paradox, I suppose, and what better example than the story of the caves?

What caves?

You don't remember?

Nope.

It was summer and we were in the south of France.

You were five years old. We decided to go and visit the *Grotte des Demoiselles.*

You didn't want to go. You had other plans: build a Lego ship, find a lizard, save the world or mope around. Who knows? One would have thought that going underground into the largest cave in the world, a cave full of giant stones shaped like animals and monsters, would have thrilled you.

But no, not you.

We dragged you along, of course, and once on the road, you were back to your smiling, happy self. We played *il ou elle* - a game of guessing who a person is by asking questions to which only a yes or no answer is permitted - and we played it goofy with improbable questions and unexpected people!

We left the seaside and were now driving north through the wine country, following the river up to the lovely village of Saint-Martin where we stopped for lunch, and where you jumped into the fountain in the square. Then we drove farther north to the grottos.

The countryside there isn't much to look at. We were not quite inside the *National Park des Cévennes* with its contrasted landscape of narrow valleys and jagged ridges, desolate plateaus and lonesome peaks, and we had just left the *garrigue*, a land of wild lavender and thyme, of stunted oaks, all of it soaked in a continuous cacophony of cicadas' songs. We were between two geological worlds, in a country of isolated ...

Enough with the description already, please!

At the entrance to the cave we joined a tour guide and a group of about twenty other visitors. We followed the guide inside to the spectacular *Cathédrale des Abîmes.*

It's no wonder the main cave is called that. Imagine descending into a huge chamber, sixty meters deep, filled with tall columns rising from many different floor levels and with draperies of limestone hanging free from rock ceilings. The cold was suddenly biting, and as we slowly made our way down the narrow stone staircase, you began to complain that you were tired, that you wanted Glenn to carry you.

"No," Glenn said sternly, but you continued to whine. And whine. Mildly exasperated, Glenn pulled you firmly ahead, farther down the stairs.

Adrian and I stayed behind on the third landing with the rest of the group to listen to the guide. Then, as we slowly made our way down to the next level, I heard a plump, middle-aged woman just ahead of me mutter something about *un enfant mal traité* - a maltreated child.

Leaning to her left, I saw you slumped against the railing, your face red as you stared stubbornly at Glenn, who was now trying to make you stand up. I held Adrian back who by now was rolling his eyes, embarrassed for us all. We waited as the tour guide and the rest of the group passed you by. For some reason, the plump middle-aged woman had waited with us and now followed us as we caught up with you.

"Monsieur!" she called out to Glenn.

Glenn looked up, surprised. "*Oui?*"

"Monsieur," she repeated with some fervor, "I have been a teacher of children for the last thirty years and..." All of this in French. As you know, your father speaks French well enough, but not under stress. Glaring at her, he kept it short.

"*Et quoi?*" - and what?

"Well," the woman went on, slightly miffed, "your child here seems to me to be quite distraught and..."

"Why don't you mind your own business, lady?" Glenn retorted in broken French, which was really funny, but we were not laughing.

"I do believe," the woman insisted, looking around as if to find support, and she found me - "Now, Madame, don't you think that this boy here looks, well, unkempt?"

I looked into her small eyes and then down at you, and suddenly, in the harsh light of the landing, I saw exactly what she saw: a skinny five-year-old in a rumpled T-shirt three sizes too big - you had insisted on wearing Adrian's and then soiled it at lunch while splashing around in the fountain. You wore dirty, untied high tops completely out of season and out of local fashion. Your hair was long and messy. You did look disheveled. On top of that, you were sitting on the floor with your head bent forward, your arms hugging your chest as if recoiling from danger, as if you were being or had been - what, *tabassé* or beaten up?

And then it dawned on me. You knew exactly what you were doing! You knew the woman was concerned and upset at Glenn, and you were playing her! You were playing us all!

The woman, of course, didn't get it. How could she have? She was still trying to engage Glenn, but he had enough. Telling her to shut up in full English this time, he picked you up, threw you over his shoulder and turned to leave. The woman stood there speechless, as Adrian and I watched your face over Glenn's shoulder.

Having gotten what you wanted, that is being carried

up and out of there, you were now grinning with joyful satisfaction, giving a thumbs up, and looking like an angel.

I don't remember any of this, but what I do know is that I didn't like caves.

Come on, Dylan! You turned your own bedroom into one! Shades down and no light on except for the glow of your laptop, piles of dirty clothes all over the floor, fitted sheet off one or two corners of the bed. Why couldn't your OCD be about extreme neatness and tidiness?

Mom! Only psychopaths have that type of OCD.

In movies, yes, but not always in real life. It would have been pleasant, for a change, to encounter tidiness when I walked into your bedroom!

It would have freaked you out, trust me. As for the dark bedroom, it was much later, in high school. Until then, I had plenty of light and colors. I covered the walls and ceiling with graffiti, remember?

I loved your graffiti. They were inspiring. And I dearly miss those years, Dylan. They were your boyhood years and your most creative despite the fact that you had a lousy art teacher.

She would let us know when she had her periods so we would watch out for her temper. She also knew how to scream real good!

Why be different from the rest of those French teachers?

Don't start trashing the Academy, please!

I am not trashing anything. Just stating the facts. I am still very much conflicted about it, you know? Reeling at times about your spending eleven years there.

Why? Adrian did!

Adrian was better equipped to cope with it.

You mean he wasn't a retard.

I mean no such thing and you damn well know it! The traditional French way of learning suited Adrian well enough, and it didn't suit you, that's all. The French academic system is so rigid in its rules that there was no room to accommodate you. Not to mention that making the process of learning enjoyable isn't a value in French pedagogy. Let's be honest, Dylan. You mostly had semi-despotic French teachers who refused to see that not all children learn the same way.

Mom! The science teacher in middle school was the most fucked up of them all, and she was American! She was so mean she had a huge kind of traffic light planted on her desk. When it flashed green, we were allowed to ask questions. When it flashed red, we weren't allowed to breathe.

Trust the French to hire an American with a *bleu-blanc-rouge* personality.

Bleu-blanc-rouge?

The French flag.

Very funny.

Not really. I swear that by third grade you were associating reading and writing with pain, and that from then on, your academic life was a misery.

Do you have to be so dramatic about it? I wouldn't call my time at the Academy a misery.

But it was. I insist that it was. You were so frustrated that by the time you finished elementary school, I was the one doing most of your homework.

Which made you miserable, not me!

Good one! Still, nothing to laugh about. You really

were struggling, Dylan. That's why we got you tested in the first place. As a result, a couple of teachers in middle school - yes, it took that long! - accommodated you well enough, like allowing you to present a short film instead of an essay on any given subject, such as...

...Yellow journalism in social studies! I remember that.

You also made one on the Holocaust that was very moving, even though in the process you almost set fire to the basement while burning up a giant star of David you had cut out of yellow cardboard.

In sixth grade, your history teacher tested you orally at recess instead of in writing. She was one of these unique gifted educators, thoughtful, insightful ...

And French!

...probably because being the heiress to an old family fortune, she didn't actually need to work, and only taught because she *liked* it. Of course, she left at the end of the year to return home. Consequently, it was Monsieur, freshly arrived from France, who took over her post as history teacher of the middle school.

I hated Monsieur. He was lucky he left right at the end of the school year because I had decided to trash his bicycle and throw dog shit in his letter box. That's how much I hated him. He made me feel like a total retard.

Did you know that he'd actually wanted to go to Egypt, but having found no open position there he had reluctantly taken his last choice of postings abroad - Berkeley. As soon as he got here, he let it be known that he despised both American culture, capitalistic in nature, and private schools where parents refused to mind their own business. The way he saw it, we thought of ourselves as almighty, a wealthy bunch paying a lot of money to dictate our will to educators such as himself.

You have to bear in mind that traditionally in France, parents have no say in their children's education. Teachers are autocratic figures, and one does not challenge them, or even discuss their decisions. You drop your child outside the school gates in the morning and pick him or her up after school, and that's about it. You do not meet with a teacher unless asked to.

Within a few weeks in Monsieur's seventh grade class, you were both defeated, and dispirited.

Mostly I was angry. So angry that I couldn't focus on anything he said.

Whatever you succeeded in learning by heart was so poorly spelled that all your test results were catastrophic. And since he also took a point off for each missing accent,...

That was vicious!

...your average score was three out of ten. And yes, that was quite vicious.

At the end of the second month, just as classes were over, I walked into Monsieur's classroom. After his initial shock at seeing an uninvited mom, and probably remembering his minimal training in American parent-teacher interactions, he listened. He listened with the face of someone trying hard to feign some indulgence. I explained about your dyslexia and suggested - gasp! - that your memorization in French of our long history was probably sufficient and could, at the very least, be acknowledged. That perfect spelling and accentuation in that subject were, perhaps, not essential. That instead of penalizing those who got an accent wrong, he could reward those who got it right?

Monsieur responded by first offering me the tight smile of someone who knew with whom he was dealing. Then, fussing over some papers on his desk, he reminded me that he had been teaching for over fifteen years. Finally, having squared up all his papers, he informed me with some hauteur that he'd immediately recognized the kind of mother I was.

"And what kind would that be?" I asked, already livid.

"*Une mère qui veut des privilèges!* A mother who wants privileges, that's what!" he retorted, standing up. Oh, he had met many, many such mothers indeed! And he also knew all about this learning differences business. "The latest excuse parents have found to justify the laziness and stubbornness of their children!"

I didn't slap him. I didn't slap him and I should have. I didn't slap him and I am still pissed off at myself for not doing it.

You failed that class and never discovered the pleasure of studying history. For someone blessed with a huge imagination and always starved for fables and stories, what a terrible shame that was! As for Monsieur, he indeed left the school at the end of that year, at long last posted where he wanted to be, somewhere in the developing world where no mother would ever dare question his pedagogic skills.

I had a great French teacher that year.

Okay. A good one out of what? Twenty-five or so?

Mom, stop! Why don't you accept the fact that I was not unhappy there? Why don't you understand that it was my school, my world. I had all my friends there. Sure, I didn't like some teachers, but who did? I was

56

struggling, and there wasn't much they could have done. I learned differently, yes? I learned things in "wholes" — I was told — and most tests are based on retaining parts, like in multiple choices. I hated those fucking tests!

Dylan, please! Stop with that language.

I couldn't fix my brain on them. I couldn't think. I didn't even go by gut feeling. Instead, you know what I did? You want to know what I did to fill the hour when we were being tested?

Tell me.

I played a game. On the first question I'd check (a) as answer. Second question I'd check (b) and so forth. Then I would start ticking the answers from (d) all the way back to (a). I would also do (d) (a) (c) (b) at random for a change of pace, I was so bored! I never actually looked at the answers, not even at the questions! Don't get me wrong. I am pretty sure I tried the first time we had such a test, since I was a good boy who didn't know he was retarded.

Dylan!

What?

Stop saying that. Stop putting yourself down.

Why not?

Because it hurts me, damn you!

The way I understand it, in test taking, retards like me prefer essay questions, but since I was also dyslexic, my writing sucked. See? I was fucked right and left. And by the way, Mom, having me tested didn't help with the problems. It only gave them a name. It wasn't the Academy's fault, either. I would have faced the same shit anywhere. So stop chewing on it, okay?

I am not chewing on it. I am only revisiting the entire

sad story because it's all I've got, and it's good for me to think it through and put it into words. I am also looking back on it with a different set of eyes. Of course, you would have faced the same challenges in any other school, I know that! But perhaps the American system, with a single language to deal with and its appreciation of differences in the learning process, would have better suited you?

No system would have helped. The school for dummies you sent me to the last two years of high school didn't help.

Yes, it did! Yes, it did! Why are you being so hypocritical? May I remind you that you were expelled from your regular high school? That we didn't have much choice, and that this particular school was a saving grace? The classes were small, the teachers kind and accommodating. They gave you all the time you needed for your SAT, which, by the way, was all about multiple choices, and you got good results. That school wasn't for dummies, as you so rudely put it, but for teens with learning differences.

Same thing.

Not! What's the matter with you?

You said we would not speak about high school yet, and here you are again talking about high school. I hate it.

Okay. Let's take another break.

SIX

Do you remember Jean-Philippe, your teacher in both kindergarten and second grade? He came to see me a few months after you'd left.

I liked him. He was nice. He never screamed, and he let us do art whenever we wanted.

Except that you didn't say "art" but "lard!" You'd ask, "*on peut faire du lard,* please?" - can we make lard? which cracked him up since in French the expression *faire du lard* or *to make lard* means to loaf around. How could he resist you?

He called himself Jean-Tulipe although we didn't know it was a flower! Then again, he was gay.

Dylan!

Oh, Mom, I'm just saying that to get you going. We were six-year-old kids. We knew he was gay because the older kids on the playground called him gay behind his back, but we had no idea what it meant! When I asked about it, I was told that it meant he liked guys! Since most girls around were really annoying, that made sense to me. Can we speak about something else now, please?

How about pagodas?

Pagodas? Where is that coming from?

As I said, Jean-Philippe came to visit and we talked — no, not talked but mused about your sociability and imagination. That's when he reminded me of the pagoda story. In kindergarten, after the Christmas break, he'd asked you all to share your "holiday special moment," and you had done so with — how shall I put it? — with a certain creativity.

When I picked you up that afternoon after class, Jean-Philippe chided me gently by exclaiming, "You never told us you were going to China!"

I didn't understand.

"China?"

"*Oui,* China. Dylan told us all about it today."

"What do you mean?"

"You didn't go to China?"

"*Mais non!* Are you telling me that Dylan told the class we spent Christmas in China?"

"And quite well! He described the pagodas, told us about the food..."

The part about the food made sense. You loved Chinese food, but *pagodas?* I was mystified. I thought you must have seen something about China on TV.

"He must have seen something about China on TV," I said.

"Sesame Street in Beijing?! Ah! Dylan." Jean-Philippe laughed, and there it was, all packed up in that laughing "ah!" Your imagination, your world of make believe, your mischievousness, your youthful extravagance.

Given that episode, I shouldn't have been surprised when, a few weeks later, I got a phone call from the mother of Jeremy, one of your classmates. You had spent the night at their house, and she had driven you both back to school the following morning. I hadn't met her yet. A French-speaking mother from Belgium, she was, like me, a fresh addition to the Academy community.

"I just wanted to tell you how very sorry we all are about James," she said gently.

"James?" I asked, dumbfounded.

"Yes, Dylan told us about him last night at dinner, and I was so moved that I thought I'd call you. You don't mind, do you?"

Should I mind? I wondered.

"What did Dylan say?" I asked, cautiously.

"*Et bien*, he told us about James, and I felt terrible. I didn't know you'd lost a son and..."

"Waitwaitwait!" I interrupted. "You're *not* telling me that Dylan told you he has a dead brother called James, are you?"

"*Mais si!* That's exactly what he told us. And how you were still grieving and — I mean, he didn't put it like that, of course, but it was obvious that he was sad and worried for you."

I groaned. I groaned, and then I sighed the heaviest sigh of all the heavy sighs ever breathed.

"There isn't any James!" I finally managed to say, feeling all at once embarrassed and unsurprised — thinking of the pagodas.

"What do you mean?" she asked, suddenly confused.

"What I mean is that Dylan made it all up. He has a brother yes, an older brother. That brother is very much alive and his name is Adrian."

"I know. Dylan told us about him, too."

"Well, I suppose that's a good thing." I laughed. "Dylan, you see, has an hyperactive imagination! I am sorry that ..."

"Oh, don't apologize," she interrupted, dismissing the awkwardness. "Kids will be kids! I have to say, though, that when he told us James was buried in your backyard, it made me wonder a little. But I never questioned for a minute the core of the story!"

Today, it's Adrian who has his brother's ashes buried in the garden. Eerie, wouldn't you say?

Disturbing.

Perhaps. As if the death of one brother had been preordained. As if, within you, it had already been written. As if you told the story of James so it wouldn't be you.

That afternoon, when I picked you up after school I asked, "Would you like to tell me about James?"

"Oh." You giggled. "Jeremy's mom believed me, didn't she? I am the best at stories!"

"That, you are. But why *James*?"

"I dunno." You shrugged. "Because of the movie?"

"Which movie?" And then it came to me. Of course. *James and the Giant Peach!* A few weeks earlier we had gone to the theater to see it but had never gotten to the end, nor to the middle for that matter. You were bored within twenty minutes, and we had left in a hush.

Bored. Is that the right word to describe your mind? A mind on the fast track and in a constant state of boredom? Boredom or restlessness? Can one be bored and not restless? Can one be restless without being bored? No matter. You were who you were, intensely drawn to things and then, as intensely, uninterested in them. You couldn't explain why. That is until a few years later, in the sixth grade I believe, when you called me to your room and, pointing at an acronym on your computer screen, you announced, *Here, Mom, I have that. It says it right here. I have ADHD.*

As you read out loud the list of symptoms it represented, I saw how relieved you were to have found a name for your agitation, for your inability to focus or finish whatever it was you started, for your overloaded mind.

As you spoke, I saw the toddler you had been, sitting between my legs on the floor with a pile of picture books on the side. I would pick one up and begin to read, but after three or four pages you'd grab it shut, and pick the next one to which you would to the exact same thing. I don't believe we ever finished a book.

Then again, perhaps I never found the right story for you. We should have taken off, I think, you and me, hand in hand, and gone through all the bookstores and libraries in town, and then in the next town, and the next, and all the towns of all the countries in the entire wide world, until we found the book for you. Until we found the story that would engage you and keep you still and un-bored, until you found your peace.

But we never did. We never took off and you never found your peace.

Later, it would be the same with the arts. You went through them all at the speed of light: pottery, woodcarving, drawing, welding, blacksmithing, and whatever else. A few classes on, and you were done.

Likewise with physical activities. Between the age of six and twelve you tried just about everything there was to try: karate, aikido, gymnastics, rock-climbing, kickboxing. Each time, within days or weeks you had enough.

See? You said earlier that if you'd known what was coming you would have put me into sports. You did put me into sports. It didn't work.

These were combat sports, fitness and team activities. I see now that they weren't for you. In such settings, you couldn't keep your focus. You wanted to follow your own rules at your own pace on your own terms and, since you couldn't, you became restless. No, when I said sports, I meant one of endurance like running, because running is a high. When you run, your brain turns itself off, your body produces endorphins, which is a natural morphine. It triggers a good feeling in your body, gives you a sense of euphoria. You would have gotten hooked, Dylan, no doubt about that.

That's why, had I known what I know now about the disorders that would come to plague and destroy you, I would have hired a private coach to train you three, four times a week since an early age, to train you until you could no longer *not* run.

Do you remember what your track and field coach in high school told me one afternoon, as I was waiting for you at the edge of the field? I'm sure I told you.

I don't remember. What did he say?

He first asked me where you had trained before, and when I told him that you had never trained anywhere, that you hated running and even walking, he was flabbergasted. He said that you were an incredible runner, a natural, and that if you stuck it out, you would go far. I looked at you again and I believed him.

You were flying.

**

And so, I am wondering. What was going on in your mind while you were in high school, Dylan? Were you at all worried about your lack of self-control?

Worried? I don't know. I don't think so. I was mostly frustrated. Frustrated and totally uninterested in what they were teaching me. I hated math and I hated religious studies. The teachers were annoying. Annoying and uptight and mean, and they weren't even French!

Not funny, Dylan.

They didn't inspire me, and obviously I didn't inspire them to inspire me! And so, I was anxious, but being anxious was also who I was all the time, everywhere. I didn't know any other way of being, so what could I do or say? My mind kept getting distracted all on its own, distracted and edgy, ready to fly out of my head. I just couldn't contain it. And then it would just shut down. I don't remember it ever being otherwise. I don't remember ever being comfortable in a classroom.

That's why I mentioned Jean-Philippe. When he came to see me, he told me that in kindergarten you were already fidgety, and that in second grade you began developing facial tics when you had to write the sentences he was dictating. It was obvious to him that you were struggling with the writing process, but he thought it was just a matter of time. He knew, just as we did, that children develop differently and at different paces. You'd catch up in time.

You kept soldiering on, but by age seven you were having these same tics at home.

I took it lightly. Lots of kids have tics, I told myself. I, too, had a facial tic at that age. I even had some weird rituals going, such as switching the light on and off six times before going to sleep.

You outgrew it, though!

I did. I also outgrew my resistance to learning, as I like to call my academic shortcomings in primary school. To this day, I can taste the sticky, sour feeling of it. The sudden fog, the lockdown inside my mind when whatever the teacher was saying would *not* - could not hook itself inside my brain. I am also pretty sure I wasn't interested in whatever she was yapping on about. Still, I don't recall ever feeling guilty or ashamed about my academic shortcomings. I was happy when my friend, Martine, was at the top of the class, and sorry when she was second to Monique, which quite distressed her.

As for me, I always was second or third to the last. *Il faut la secouer comme un prunier* read the comment of a teacher on a school report. "She needs to be shaken like a plum tree."

A plum tree?

Yes. Of all trees, a plum tree. It was both funny and humiliating. The ensuing fallen plums being, I suppose, my inattention, my disruption, my ineptitude. In other words, my shortcomings.

In fifth grade, *mademoiselle ma maîtresse*, an old spinster always dressed in green - brownish green, yellowish green, blueish green, and greenish green - let my mother stand in the rain at the bottom of the stairs leading to the porch where she stood outside her classroom, while informing her that, in her educated opinion, I should prepare to end elementary school and be sent to a vocational one to learn a trade. Hairdressing perhaps, or sewing. Sewing would be good. Something I could do with my hands, since my intellect...well, and there she hesitated, coughing a little. Or did she? How would I know? I wasn't there, but I can well imagine. One always coughs a little when one brings terrible news to a mother, no? *Et bien,* she said, *vous comprenez, n'est-ce pas?*

No. My mother did not understand. Not in the least. Her daughter wasn't stupid! Her daughter couldn't possibly be stupid. She wasn't even eleven years old! How can you decide the fate of an eleven-year-old when her intellect is not yet fully developed? How can you cut her off entirely from academia, and on top of that, announce it with a sour face!

Your grandmother was so upset that she did the unthinkable. She went straight to the headmistress, something unheard of in those ancient days when teachers were kings, when mothers did *not* meet with them or with the headmistress unless they were asked to. My mother? She walked right into her office and demanded to be heard.

Madame la directrice was a good and powerful woman. She stood tall and strong, and unsmiling. She didn't patrol the corridors often but when she did, we knew our places. *Here comes Berthe au grand pied!*

someone would whisper and we would scatter away or stand at attention.

Why did you call her that?

Bigfoot Bertha? Because of her name. Let me explain: *Bigfoot Bertha* was the nickname given to King Charlemagne's mother, and don't ask why because it never was officially recorded. There are many stories about it, of course, and a few good legends, but as with the Bible, who knows what's what.

As for our *directrice,* her last name was Berthomieu and being very tall, she had big feet. You can see why the students called her Bigfoot Bertha behind her back.

This formidable woman actually cared a great deal for us girls and proved to have, for the times, a good sense of child development. She also had a bit of the mind of a philosopher. She told my mother, "A little light often lasts the night while a big one sometimes burns itself out before dawn. You'll see," she went on reassuringly, "Dominique will blossom in middle school. With a new teacher at each course, she will be challenged in many different ways, and I believe that's what she needs. Let's try a year, shall we?"

She was right. From sixth grade on, I never once failed again. I had to study harder than most because I, too, had a difficult time retaining information, but I succeeded.

So, Mom, you were ADD?

Something like that. There was no name for it back then, just as there was no name for learning differences, no name or even studies about what a right brainer or a left brainer can or cannot do. Only the word dyslexia existed, and my brother was diagnosed with it in the late

Sixties, when he was ten years old. He wrote phonetically. He saw what we call in French an "*orthophoniste*," a person who specializes in re-educating students with such a disorder.

A speech therapist. Did it help?

It did psychologically, when she assured him that one day, he would not need to write anything down since he would have a secretary to do it for him. Kind, clever woman! He still can't spell, by the way, but as you know he is a very successful businessman, and as the speech therapist told him, he now has a secretary, not to mention a computer, to do all the spelling checks he needs.

I wasn't bad at spelling, was I?

You weren't bad in English when you paid attention, but since paying attention was in itself a struggle...

I was fucked, any which way you looked at it.

I wish you'd stop with the F-word, Dylan. It's getting to me.

The F-word is the only word that fits the way it was, Mom. The way I felt. Admit it, ok? Admit it for once?

... ...

Mom?

Okay.

Say it then. Say, Dylan was fucked anyway you looked at it.

Dylan...

Say it!

Dylan was fucked anyway you looked at it.

Thanks. Now you can go back to my dyslexia.

Which manifested in the decoding of words. Managing two languages certainly didn't help!

I hated reading.

I know. I could see how long it took you to read even the shortest stories. You didn't complain because you were sweet, but you didn't like it!

Did you ever confront your fifth-grade teacher, the one who said you should be taken out of school to learn sewing?

I didn't, but your grandmother did! Years later she arranged to get an appointment at her hairdresser at the same time that *la femme* in green was having her perm done. They had been sharing the same stylist for years but had never acknowledged each other.

That afternoon, Mamie tapped happily on Mademoiselle's shoulder and asked if she remembered her daughter, Dominique, "the little girl who couldn't? The little girl whose intellect was limited?"

Mademoiselle nodded a curt *oui* and a polite how is she doing?

To which my mother retorted grandly that I had never been able to learn a trade since I was still hopeless at doing things with my hands, but that I had just obtained my baccalaureate in economics and was on my way to college. Sweet, sweet vindication! She tasted it on her lips like a delicacy!

And when she got home, she poured herself a small glass of Petit Chablis and toasted, as she reported to me later, to the thin lips and tight ass of Mademoiselle my fifth-grade teacher.

"*I love Mamie!*"

Yes, that Mamie was pretty cool.

"*Why* that *Mamie? Was there any other?*"

As I told you before, she had many sides to her, your

grandmother. We all do. As we grow older, we shed some and grow new ones. I was her young daughter. Her psychology was way above my head, as it was supposed to be, and so I both loved and resented her. Don't all kids resent their mothers at some point or another? Didn't you?

Not really, no.

Oh, come on, Dylan! You always asked me not to embarrass you in front of your friends! And so did your brother. As a matter of fact, he still does!

Well, you can be pretty intense, Mom! And seriously opinionated!

Which, I'll admit, can be embarrassing, but there you go, that's who I am. As for Mamie, I certainly loved her when she stood up to such conceited teachers as Mademoiselle. Today I wonder how many French mothers let their daughters be taken out of general education because a teacher so decreed!

It would have been the same for me, yes?

Had you lived in those days? Absolutely. Except that instead of sewing, masonry work would have been suggested.

Did I believe that what had been true of me would be true of you? Did I believe you would outgrow your tics — the twitching of the neck, the blinking of the eyes — and your difficulties with reading, and find your way academically? That it would take one person, one teacher to inspire you? One teacher to trust you, and you would trust yourself? Of course, I did, but then again I was your mother. When it comes to your own, as aware as you are, you in fact see very little. I learned that the hard way.

SEVEN

Christmas

Christmas was sweet and melancholy. You were always the one putting the tree together for me, with some reluctance in the last years to be sure, but you did it, and I missed that. So, I put the tree together with Mamie, and I cried. I cry often since you left. For a long time, I cried in the street seeing bus number eighteen that you took to Jack London Square to go work at your dad's office. And then one day, number eighteen disappeared to be replaced by number thirty-three, and I cried because I missed number eighteen, and how dare the city take it away from me?

I still cry hearing the Bart train coming in from the suburbs at Rockridge Station where I used to pick you up when you returned from seeing friends. I cry looking at Manouche and at Lili...

My cat.

Your cat. We chose her together just over a year before you left. We brought her home, and she made the closet in your room her nest, burrowing away inside the pile of dirty clothes. Given her crazy purring, she must have loved the stink of them!

Mom ...

I am wondering who will bury her when the time comes, and who will bury Manouche. You were the one who, over the years, helped me bury all our pets.

You loved animals, and you cared for them. You loved and cared for them just as you loved and cared for children and old people because like you, animals, children and old people live in the now and in the imagination.

You were the kid, the teen, the young man who helped old ladies cross the street, who engaged them in conversation, who was curious about their lives. We would be driving through town and you would ask me to stop so you could get out and help someone! As for your love of animals, it was quite endearing.

I get that from you. So does Adrian.

Yes, but you are the one who brought that love into action.

I did?

You did. Don't you remember Ceci?

Tchi-Tchi?

Yes. You spell it one way and pronounce it another. In any case, you were three years old when, one late afternoon, Adrian, you, Gypsy, and I walked down the street to visit Vincente and Maria, the Italian gardeners who had, a few weeks earlier, given your brother the puppy, Gypsy.

And?

The family was gathered in the basement that was also their summer kitchen. Claudio, their twenty-year-old son, sat in the wheelchair to which he had been confined since he was beaten up by gang members in high school a couple of years earlier. Claudio's passion was parrots and crows.

That evening a tall white parrot was perched on his shoulder. Further into the darkness of the basement, on top of an old and silent grandfather clock, stood a large stuffed crow with its beak wide open, one scrawny leg stretched out, its talons in ruin. Creepy. I kept close to Maria, by the stove where she was cooking a summer stew. Vincente and Adrian were outside in the yard with Gypsy.

And?

Suddenly, Claudio, who had just rolled his wheelchair out of the basement, screamed, "Ceci! Where is Ceci? Who opened her cage?"

Silence. I stepped outside and stared at the open cage where another of Claudio's parrots had been happily chatting a few minutes earlier.

"It wasn't me!" you called out from behind me.

I sighed, turned around, and with my eyes boring into yours and my arms folded (why do we always fold our arms when scolding a child?) I asked, "Why did you open the cage?"

"You always said!" you shot back, folding your arms right back at me.

We were like two bulls facing each other.

"I always said what?" I demanded.

"To open all the bird cages. You always said!" you repeated, yelling now. Then, looking at your brother, "Didn't she? Didn't she?" and back to me, sourly insistent, "You said!"

"You did," Adrian confirmed. "You even told us how

you opened one yourself when you were a kid."

I closed my eyes and silently regrouped before making you apologize to Claudio.

Claudio who, your brother would later tell me, had a deck of cards with porn on them! Adrian had picked them up from the TV stand, thinking he would play cards like he did with Mamie, before looking at them and throwing them onto the floor.

I didn't like Claudio. He played with porn cards, and he put parrots and crows in cages. When they died, he stuffed them. And yes, I did tell you and your brother that no animal should ever be locked up. Yes, I did open a cage myself, once.

What happened, Mom, and where? How old were you?

It was at home. I was six or seven years old. That summer, Papi and Mamie had been given a couple of turtledoves to raise for food. The cage stood on a large, tall bench in the garden, under the cherry tree. I remember how hot the afternoon was. It must have been a Sunday since my father was not working. He and Mamie were taking a nap.

I was supposed to do the same, but I had left my bedroom to come and see the turtledoves. They were white with a black ring around their necks, and I thought they were the prettiest things in the world. I stood there looking at them, and the more I looked the less I wanted them to be killed, and cooked, and eaten.

So, I pulled myself up onto the bench, lifted the top of the cage and let it fall on its side. I stood still, fascinated by what I had done, and waited to see if the doves would fly away. They did. All at once, they took off side by side, and I saw them soar into the air, high above the cherry tree.

Wow! And then what did you do?

I ran back to my bedroom, of course, and kept quiet. It took forever, or so it seemed to me, for my parents to get up and the next thing I knew, my father was looming over me with that very seriously upset look on his face. I don't quite remember how it went down from there, but down it went!

Were you grounded?

I was grounded. I could no longer go out and run around the hills with my friends at night while my parents played *pétanque* on the square down below with the neighbors.

Were you grounded for long?

It seemed like forever, but it probably was only a couple of days. For one thing, Mamie was rather happy about what had happened. She wasn't keen on killing and eating doves either. As for my father, being a nonconformist, he probably quietly rejoiced in having a rebellious daughter.

Did you punish me for opening the cage at the porn weirdo house?

The porn weirdo house? My goodness, Dylan, the things you choose to retain!

The things you choose to tell me!

A good point. No, I didn't punish you. It would have been hypocritical, don't you think? You did what you believed was right, although setting birds free should be a very carefully thought out decision because back in the wild they seldom survive. I should have told you as much, so that one is on me.

As far as Ceci was concerned, everyone agreed that he couldn't have flown very far. We all went down the street and around the block, calling "Ceci! Ceci!" some of us with an Italian accent and some of us with a French one, but night was falling and Ceci was probably holding still somewhere in a tree, freedom-dazzled.

I decided that Adrian, you, and I would go home and make flyers announcing a reward for Ceci. Two days later, while you were at school, a woman called to tell me excitedly that her young daughter had just spotted a small green parrot sitting right outside their window, in a willow tree.

Why wasn't she at school?

The little girl? How would I know? Maybe she was sick or home schooled and who cares? I swear, Dylan, you have the weirdest concerns!

I drove straight to Maria and Vincente to pick up Claudio and his wheelchair. We drove three streets down to a cul-de-sac where we parked in the middle of the circle that ended it. I got Claudio's chair out of the car, unfolded it and helped him into it. We looked up and around as he called Ceci. Sure enough, within minutes the little green bird flew out of the willow tree, and onto his shoulder.

And then back in its cage. That sucks! What was the reward?

A hundred dollars. The little girl sent me a note to thank me, adding that the money would go toward the savings she had to buy a violin. I thought that was wonderful.

Yes, and she didn't have to go to school.

Dylan!

***

How about Lolita? Do you remember Lolita?

Your cat? Vaguely. What happened? Did I mess up?

On the contrary. You were seven when, on a rainy day, we took her to the vet to put her to sleep. At almost eighteen, she had become quite senile. We brought her back in a towel, and you dug the hole in which we laid her down. I remember that it started raining, but you didn't stop. You went on digging until the job was done. Lolita the cat was gone.

I buried Miss Rosie, too.

Yes, you did. Years later. You buried her with the ashes we had kept of Gypsy who was, by then, gone a year.

You sat me on the porch, poured me a glass of white wine and grabbed the pickaxe. You dug in silence while I drank my wine. You dug for Miss Rosie, our eight-year-old guinea-pig and the smartest, sassiest guinea-pig of all the smart and sassy guinea-pigs in the world.

And in all the other worlds.

And in all the other worlds.

How disquieting it now feels, since Glenn buried your ashes in the garden. He dug a hole among the tall, red kangaroo paws, beneath the statue of the young Buddhist monk you had once carried there for me. We chose that spot because of the monk's smaller self sitting on the bird feeder on the way down to the front gate. Every time you walked by, you rubbed his head. For good luck, you told me.

As if luck cared! It certainly wasn't at your side on April 29, 2014. Neither was the monk's spirit. That afternoon, you died alone in the blistering heat of a dark room the size of a closet in a dilapidated flat, deep in the belly of the city's poorest side, away from the light.

Where all the messed-up souls go to end their fucked-up lives.

I never said that!

Not like that. But something similar when Little Stevie overdosed there.

Mea Culpa, Dylan. He was your friend, and I didn't want to hear. I was wrong and judgmental. I know better now, don't I? And it's not a pretty feeling.

EIGHT

Each fall, several mothers of girls in your grade organized a mother-daughter weekend trip to Castanoa, a resort on the protected California coastline. Since you were quite popular among the girls, their mothers invited us and one other boy, your best friend, to join them that October. You were all fifth graders. We slept in tent bungalows, picnicked on the beach, hiked in the afternoon. In the evening, while we mothers drank Champagne, you kids ran around the camp doing what kids do.

That Saturday morning you asked me for some money to buy a moon ring at the resort's gift shop.

"A moon ring?" I asked, surprised.

To which you answered happily, "Yes, it's for Simone."

Shortly after, there was a loud buzz coming from the gathered girls, and then great excitement as they waited for you to give the ring to your fairest of all.

She had been in your grade since kindergarten, but it was the first year she was in your class, and now she had a ring on her finger. I thought that was the sweetest thing.

On that school year picture, you sit at the end of the front row, and she is standing at your shoulder on the second row. You were both nine years old.

I liked Simone a lot, but she was too uptight for me so it didn't last.

What do you mean, too uptight?

She would not let me kiss her.

That's not being uptight! That's being a good little girl.

Oh, Mom! What do you know?

Obviously not what *you* know.

For months after you were gone, I couldn't see any of your old French Academy classmates without falling apart. They were all such a part of your history. You had grown up together, practically as siblings, and just like siblings, you had cared and bickered and competed with one another mercilessly.

You drifted away from them in high school, but they held you dear in their hearts, and were terribly affected by your death. They called from all over the country, and Jeremy flew in from New York to hug me. They emailed one another and they emailed me, so sadly and beautifully that it broke my heart all over again. The few who still lived in town gathered at Jeremy's when he came home to remember you. Elsewhere, friends met in a park and released twenty-three balloons into the skies with your name written on each one of them.

You were gone eight months when I saw Simone again. Glenn, your grandmother, and I were dining in a Thai restaurant when she suddenly materialized in front of me. I hadn't seen her in years and here she stood, a vibrant twenty-three-year-old young woman, smiling and bending down to kiss me. I fell apart. I just couldn't take it in — that she was here and you were not. That you would never again be part of her life, or of anyone else's.

Months later, after exchanging a couple of emails, she came to see me, bringing with her a few mementos from your life at the Academy. Pictures of you with the girls, the napkin you painted for her in art class - a palm tree with pink hearts above it, a brown coconut at its foot and waves below to show that it was an island.

The sweetest thing she brought was a page of her fifth-grade diary that she had torn off for me. It read:

"I like this boy named Dylan. He is really nice to me and other people, too. He is funny and cute, too. The thing is he likes me, too. So, we're kind of like boyfriend and girlfriend."

And how lovely was that!

***

That summer, Glenn, you, and I spent a week in Maui. I think it was in June, but it could have been July. It was hot and breezy; it was heavenly. You didn't want to be there, though, and you fought us the entire time to stay in the suite at the Sheraton to watch TV and play video games. You already didn't care for the beach, for the sun, for the ocean.

Why wasn't Adrian with us?

Because he was busy working as a counselor at UC Berkeley Youth Camp, a camp you had once attended while in primary school and had lost interest in almost immediately.

Because it was all about sports, Mom! Basketball, football, baseball, swimming...

No running.

No running.

It figures.

One sport per hour. I hated it.

I know, I know, I know, but I still wish I understood why. Why you hated sports so much, so viscerally. I mean, I understand not liking one or two, but all of them? Here in America where sports are an essential part of the cultural and educational experience? You didn't even watch them on TV!

So? What is there to understand? It was the way I was, the way my body felt. An effect of my messed-up brain? I didn't even feel right walking, remember? And it wasn't laziness, as you so often said, and it grew worse with time. Or it was simply not my thing. How about that? You hate the snow, Mom, don't you? You hate the snow, and you hate the mountains. I don't try to understand why!

Because in the mountains I am claustrophobic and because the snow is cold.

Okay. You don't like the cold. Who cares why? I liked the cold. I liked the rain, too, and the snow. I liked skiing; you don't. You like deserts and you like the sea; I don't. That's just who we are. You like the sun; I liked the night. Speaking of which, it's pretty dark where I stand now, Mom, and that suits me just fine.

Does it?

***

It was also that summer that our lives changed, though we didn't recognize it at first. It all seemed so very innocent! One evening in August you went next door to watch a video with Banks, the friend you grew up with, the friend whose fifth birthday party you had upset by opening all his gifts. The movie was called *I Know What You Did Last Summer* — the story of four teens stalked by a killer one year after they covered up a car accident they were involved in. It was your first slasher film, and you got so frightened you came back home to sleep with us. I didn't think it was any big deal. It had happened to your brother when he'd watched Hitchcock's *Psycho*.

What about you? Did you ever get spooked by a movie?

Oh yes, I got spooked all right!

What was it?

Ben-Hur.

Never heard of it.

You wouldn't. It's an old 1959 movie.

That's not old, Mom, that's ancient!

Quite, but at the time it was the biggest and most expensive movie ever produced. It went on to win every award there was to win.

What was it about?

An historical drama about an enslaved Jewish prince battling the Romans in Galilee at the time of Jesus' crucifixion.

When did you see it?

In the winter of 1963, a few weeks after President

Kennedy's assassination. My best friend Nina's father had taken us both to see the film at the only theater in town, which was called The Rex. I was eleven years old, and it was my very first time at the cinema.

And the movie? What freaked you out about it?

Hold your horses. Let me remember the contest. We sat in the small, packed theater, then darkness fell and the curtain opened on a black and white newsreel about political events I neither understood nor cared about. Then, at long last, the movie began.

It was quite extraordinary, and for a long time I sat there with my mouth open, feeling all the feelings I was meant to feel and then some. It all fell apart when Ben-Hur crawled inside a lepers' cave in search of his mother and sister. I was terrified. By the time the crucifixion came, I was so small in my seat I might as well have disappeared.

I tried very hard to stick to what Nina had told me, that Jesus was just one among hundreds, that the roads leading to Jerusalem were lined with delirious men nailed up on crosses, flies going in and out of their nostrils. She'd explained that crucifying people was one of the ways the Romans executed criminals.

"What are you saying?" I'd asked, shocked. "That Jesus was a criminal?"

"If He ever *was*. And if He *was*, He surely was an agitator, a reformer - or another religious nut trying to fulfill a prophecy as old as - oh, forget it!" and she'd stopped explaining with that look on her face that said, you don't get it.

I didn't get it.

Still, the sight of that man dragging his cross through

the crowd, and of the wound on his side when He was up on the cross with blood dripping from his crown of thorns, made me feel nauseated. He might not have been whoever He was made out to be, but on screen He was still a man in agony.

For days after, I had a recurring nightmare: I am trapped in a pitch-black cellar surrounded by lepers carrying crosses on their backs. I don't see them, but I know they're there, searching for me with their half-chewed-up eyes. In a variation of that dream I can feel them brushing past me with their deformed bodies and rotting flesh, crosses banging.

I would scream then; I would scream, and Mamie would rush to my room to cradle me back to sleep, whispering, "It's all right, it's all right, it was just a bad dream, *un mauvais rêve, c'est fini,* it's over now." But the dream would linger till morning, and sometimes it stayed with me all day.

See? That's exactly what it was for me!

The difference being, Dylan, that you didn't just get spooked for a night or two. Your fright unlocked the door to Boo, and you couldn't leave our bedroom for almost a year.

Every night I lay with you and read you a story, then waited until you were asleep to leave the room. You slept surrounded by a mountain of pillows as if to protect yourself from some great danger. You were protecting yourself from your own thoughts, of course, but I didn't know that, and neither did you. You were so young!

That's when I started seeing Alison.

Yes. I can't remember now how I found her, but find her I did. A wonderful child psychologist to whom you instantly took.

She confirmed that your anxieties were mostly tied to your academic insecurities, but that you had some strong inner fear you couldn't yet verbalize. That's when you came up with a name for it: Boo. She recommended that we do some breathing exercises together before bedtime, and I remember the two of us sitting cross-legged on the rug, trying to ward off Boo. I would ask, "Where is Boo?" and you would say, "Outside, behind the door."

But Boo wasn't outside, Boo was in the bedroom with us, waiting quietly by the mountain of pillows for morning to come. He kept growing and growing until you could no longer control him.

That's when I found myself ritualizing.

Found yourself?

Yeah, found myself. I didn't think it, Mom! I didn't decide one morning to start tapping on the wall to see how it felt. It just happened, and since it gave me some relief from Boo, I kept at it.

And we didn't see a thing.

I made sure of that. Anyways, for a long time it wasn't much at all.

What did you do, aside from tapping?

Stuff, Mom. Repetitive stuff. Counting. As I said, no big deal for a long time.

That September, you started sixth grade and saw Alison once a week. You would see her on and off for the next three years. The Academy's middle school curriculum was challenging, particularly for boys, who often develop intellectually more slowly than girls. Science and social studies were taught in English, but they were at public high school level. So was English. There was French, of course, in grammar and geography and...

...history with Monsieur Asshole.

Watch your mouth!

He was an asshole, Mom, you know he was.

You can be sour about it, but you don't have to be vulgar.

You have a better word?

... ...

There. Asshole is the only word.

Enough. I don't want to be reminded of him, okay? Where was I? Ah, yes, your academic struggles. I got the books you had to read on tape and wrote most of your homework myself, imitating your tormented, pale, ant-like handwriting. Every evening, through the homework you got, I revisited the classes you had that day, all the while painfully aware of how difficult it was to get you interested. As for math...

I sucked at it.

I know, but you hung in there.

Because of Monsieur C! He was a good teacher, and a fruitcake.

You mean an eccentric.

Fruitcake, eccentric, whatever. He was also totally fair, and he was French. So, you see, not all my French teachers were evil.

You got a C+, passing the class! And that was all on you since I could not have helped there. I never got math either.

But you got a B+ in English!

Well deserved! It wasn't easy to construct my

sentences awkwardly to be believable.

It worked.

It did, and that in itself was troubling. I mean the teachers knew you, they saw your work in the classroom, they could have, should have figured it out. I was quite conflicted about that, perpetually torn between relief and anger. I was even more conflicted about my subterfuge on your behalf. Still, as you keep telling me, you were happy enough in middle school. Your closest friends were your classmates, and so were your girlfriends!

Until Gabriella.

Yes, until Gabriella. You were in the eighth grade then, and you fell seriously in love for the first time. She was a year older than you and an outsider, a freshman in high school and very pretty, with blue eyes and bouncy blonde hair. She was also brilliant.

She was so smart, everyone said she would become a brain surgeon or something! I mean, she went to Yale.

She did.

That spring, your entire grade went to France for a week in an exchange program. Earlier that year, we had hosted the French students you were now visiting. There, you tormented a few local girls and left broken hearts behind you, or so I was told. You then joined Glenn and me in the south with three of your classmates, and the parents of one. We drove to Provence together and toured the old city of Avignon, not that you cared one bit about it, but it was our last innocent summer together.

In June, you graduated from the Academy and brought Gabriella home the day before she was to leave for her own school trip to Russia. It was a warm sunny afternoon, and I watched from the deck above as you stood together by the pool, kissing and chatting. I watched as you took her in your arms and jumped in the water *tout habillés!* - with your clothes on! She laughed and you laughed with her and you were so happy it was wonderful to see!

It didn't last, did it? That winter, I cheated on her. She found out and swore to never talk to me again. She never did.

Not because you had kissed one of her girlfriends. She might have forgiven you for that. She dropped you because you had gotten drunk.

Not really...

Yes, really. When she was very young, her father had struggled with a drinking problem, and for a few years her mother had taken the children away from him. You can imagine what getting drunk meant to Gabriella. And so, she dropped you and you came home with your heart shattered, broken, in pieces. She was your first love in youth and she would be the last. You would never know love as a man - the love of a woman, the love of children.

Unfortunately, having your heart broken was just the beginning of a very long descent into the damaged world of Boo. By then, it was the middle of your second semester as a high school freshman, and everything around you was collapsing. You had lost Gabriella and were now about to be thrown off the football team.

You were thrown off the football team because you had stolen a pair of brand-new high tops in the locker room! You'd stolen them for a friend who walked proudly on campus the following morning wearing them!

It was the high tops against some weed, Mom! I already explained how I was losing it in class, how I couldn't fix my attention on anything the stupid teachers said. How I was tapping under the desk like crazy and counting in my head. I needed to chill out.

To chill out! As excuses go, that's pitiful. And how humiliating for me to be called to pick you up because you were suspended!

You felt humiliated? How did you think I felt?

I was angry, Dylan, very angry at you that day, and I couldn't go beyond that anger. Why? Because yes, it was humiliating to think I might be perceived as a failed mother, or the mother of a failed son. It was the first time I was called to come and get you, but it wouldn't be the last. I would be called again and again because you were acting up in class, because you had been caught cheating or driving a senior friend's car off the parking lot when you didn't even have a permit! I mean, Dylan, you drove a senior's car under the nose of an administrator who happened to be that senior's aunt! What were you thinking?

I wasn't thinking; I was high. I was high and unhappy and feeling like a little shit. I was tired of putting up a front. But you, the only thing you cared about was what people thought!

I cared about what people thought, yes. Of course, I did. Which mother wouldn't? The teachers, the dean, the librarian. The librarian because every time I had to pick you up that's where I'd find you — at the library. And the librarian was such a sweet woman, hugging me, trying to comfort me. She even whispered into my ear, "I know how you feel. My son was always in trouble in high school. Eventually he was expelled. And me working here, imagine that." I asked how old her son was now and she said, "Thirty-two years old." I asked how he was doing and she sighed. "Still in trouble." That brought me little comfort, I can tell you that!

As for the dean, I was in his office more times than I cared for and always defending you, justifying and explaining your actions, your behavior, practically anointing you with my trust and asking him to trust you, too. Well, guess what? I was sick of it! It had happened too many times, and I knew it wouldn't end well. I was angry.

You were always angry, Mom, which in turn made me more anxious.

There you go. We were both trapped in a circle of fear and resentment.

That's when my rituals went totally off the charts. That's when in the morning I had to put my T-shirt on a certain way, my jeans on a certain way, and my socks on with only one hand! I had to put my fucking socks on with only one hand, Mom, and tie and untie my shoelaces three times, all the while listening to you screaming for me to hurry up, that my ride was waiting, and what, in the name of God, what was taking me so long to get ready? It was hell all right, and what was I supposed to do?

Tell us about it?

I couldn't. I just couldn't. I didn't know how to explain. I thought you would think it was an act or something. I didn't understand myself why I had to do all these weird things to stop thinking weird.

Thinking weird?

Yeah. Weird shit like dying, or you dying or being killed. You found out soon enough.

Not soon enough, no, but yes, we eventually did. I'll never forget the phone call from the shrink you were meeting with. A specialist in ADHD who had given the best lecture on learning differences I had ever heard. I thought he could help. You told him about the counting, about the obsessive thoughts, and he realized pretty quickly that your problems went way beyond ADHD and dyslexia.

It was the first time ever I'd told someone, and it was the first time I'd heard about OCD. It was such a relief.

It was a relief for us, too, Dylan. That particular shrink couldn't help you, but we had a diagnosis, so now we could do something about it. We could find help!

Little did you know.

We tried, didn't we? We found a psychiatrist who put you on meds, a shrink who specialized in OCD that you began seeing twice a week. We believed we had the answer. All would be well. Soon crowds would cheer you, just like the tall gray-eyed women had predicted so many years ago in the parking lot of a supermarket.

I believed it until the next school year, your sophomore year when, mid-February, you were expelled for having been caught selling drugs on campus.

They said that and kept repeating it over and over again, but it wasn't true. I wasn't selling, Mom. I was trading weed for pills because pot wasn't helping anymore, and I...

You were selling, Dylan! How dare you still lie about that? For what purpose?

OK. OK. I sold it when I couldn't trade. It probably happened just this once, and they made a huge deal about it.

93

As they should. And I don't believe a minute it happened just this once! But go one, please.

What's crazy is that once in his office, the dean asked me to empty my pockets. In one of them, I had a Xanax and a Fentanyl. I threw them on his desk along with the rest of my stuff, and he didn't even look at them. He only took my phone while I put the pills right back in my pocket!

What an incompetent fool.

No, Mom. I was the fool. I was the fool, but I didn't care. I had my pills and in my head all was quiet.

It's quite perplexing and a bit embarrassing to think how little your father and I were aware of the spectrum of mental illnesses. Speak about parents in denial! When it came to you and your disorder, the words weren't even part of our vocabulary.

Even though Glenn has a PhD in psychology!

He does, but his specialty was social psychology, group behavior - nothing to do with clinical psychology. And so, to us, mental illnesses were other people's misery we read about or watched at the cinema. At best, they were the cheerful lunatics in the film *King of Hearts*. At worst, they were the ramblings of people who hear voices in their heads and talk to themselves out loud, or slash themselves or lose their minds because they really messed up their lives, like in the book *Ironweed*.

Mental illnesses were something tangible, something you actually saw, like a broken leg, like the sallow skin of a cancer patient, like the loss of hair, like a body in a wheelchair. Mental illnesses were not you, no way. You weren't doomed. You were sick and sick could be fixed.

Depression could be healed with love, therapy, meds, and so could anxieties and weird rituals.

It goes to show.

It does, doesn't it? The real tragedy being that, although we didn't realize it yet, beyond what we were already doing, there was nothing else to be done. Unless...

Mom?

Unless, and I fantasized quite a bit about it, unless I took you away from Oakland, away from its streets and their ready access to opioids, away from America. I should have. I should have taken you to France. Or to a foreign land. To the end of the world. To New Zealand.

Come on! What about my head? I couldn't have left it behind!

Better still, I should have taken you out of time, and brought you altogether into another era.

Gee, here you go again into fantasy land!

That's one way of looking at it. Then there is the Einstein's way. He thought that the dividing line between past, present, and future is only a stubbornly persistent illusion. Ultimately reality is timeless.

Einstein thought that?

Einstein thought that.

And?

And for you, Renaissance Italy would have worked. You could have trained as a painter or as a sculptor.

Are you crazy? Don't you remember telling me how people back then believed that those suffering from OCD were possessed by the devil, and that they had to be exorcised, not to mention locked up?

They locked up commoners, even aristocrats if their

minds were really sick, but not artists for what was perceived as oddities and eccentricities. Caravaggio is a good example of that.

Caravaggio?

A painter. A depraved genius who skirted the edges of respectability. He even killed a young man in a brawl. But the arts being at the very center of power, he got away with it. Powerful patrons made sure of that.

Doesn't sound good to me at all. Not to mention that with my luck, I would have bumped into that guy, for sure.

Not if you were far from Florence, training not as a painter or sculptor, but as a luthier.

What are you trying to do, Mom? Make me feel like fucking ignorant? What is a luthier anyway? Sounds French to me, not Italian!

It's French, yes. In Italian, the word is lituaio. A maker of string instruments. You could have studied at the Amati family's workshop in Cremona.

The Amati being?

The family who invented the violin. I can absolutely see you making one. Or a cello.

Your favorite instrument.

In classical music, yes. Don't you see yourself making one? You always loved making things with your hands. In that way you took after my father. You even studied woodcarving for a while, remember? You chiseled a tall shepherd walking stick with a removable curved tongue sticking out, close to the top. The woodcarver told me you had a natural talent, but, of course, inevitably, you soon got ...

Don't say it!

Bored.

Not. It was the teacher. She wouldn't let me do what I wanted to do, so I quit.

Why am I not surprised?

Stop! She wanted me to carve a dinner plate! A dinner plate, Mom!

What's wrong with a dinner plate?

It's dumb, that's what. I was — what, ten years old? No way I was going to carve a dinner plate. I wouldn't want to carve one now! Me? I wanted to work on a skull.

Wasn't that a bit premature? You'd just started!

So what? I felt ready!

Oh well. There was no denying your budding talent. As I said, in less hectic times, with less entertainment and fewer distractions at the tip of your fingers, you would...

And as I said, my mind would have been messed up all the same.

Medicine women in the old world had their ways of dealing with pain and oddity. Plants, brews of all sorts, and did you know? Some potions included organic opium such as laudanum and depalgos.

Strange names.

Strange names for strange ills.

There also were spells and magic, and why not? It's not like modern medicine worked for you, is it? You would have been all right. The most important thing is that, immersed in a passion with all the time in the world to grow into it, with your hands busy at work and diversions at ground zero, you would have belonged. You would have belonged and you would have lived! You would have *lived*, Dylan, I am sure of that!

I am not sure I would have liked that world. Except

for the meds with the strange names.

... ...

Mom?

... ...

Mom? Are you there?

Oh, I am here all right! I am so totally here that I am taking you there.

Where?

To Cremona.

Why?

Why not?

Because you can't, that's what. Because even as pretend it won't work. It's like, so out there!

According to whom?

Normal people?

I don't like normal. Never did. Never was. And who is to know what works and what doesn't? Who is to set parameters to the imagination? To writing? To recording? To remembering? To reality even? Not to mention to love? Because this is all about love, yes? A fierce and protective love, a love that transcends the ordinary. Here is a quote for you: "So let it be written, so let it be done," which sounds like a line from the scriptures, but is not. It's from a movie about the scriptures.

And it means?

It means that what is to be done has already been written. And I am thinking, how about the other way around? How about, "What is to be written has already been done." Time is pliable and multilayered, Dylan. It has no beginning and no end, no chronological order apart from the one we stamp on it. And when we skip its established chronology and trust in its fluidity, all its spheres interconnect.

Still. It's so ...

Out there, yes, you already said. Personally, I prefer out of the box, in the infinite possible, in the out of the ordinary and into the extraordinary. The Irish poet W.B. Yeats wrote that "the world is full of magic things, patiently waiting for our senses to grow sharper." You of all people can appreciate that. Weren't you the one with the words "Never Ordinary" tattooed in ornate blue and yellow lettering across your shoulders?

It didn't say extra...

Dylan!

Okay. Okay. And how do you propose to take me there, to this long ago, out of time land?

By writing you there, of course!

Cremona, Lombardy, April in the year 1647

In the Parish of San Faustino, the carriage came to a stop at the last dwelling of the Amati estate, on the corner of Piazza S. Domenico. The habitation stood tall at the end of the Contrada del Coltellai and the mid-afternoon sun, high and white in the sky, flashed through the thick row of poplar trees that lined the street.

Opening the door of the carriage, a woman was about to step down, her skirts and coat already gathered in her hands when she hesitated. It had obviously been raining hard because the ground was soaked and muddied. She was still hesitating when the dwelling's front door opened and a young servant called out to the coachman to drive around the back, signora, to the courtyard which is paved.

The woman withdrew inside, closed the door and the carriage brought her to a large, clean and deserted courtyard. A man came out of the house through a low-framed door and rushed to open the carriage and take the lady's hand, helping her down.

"Benvenuto, Signora Cacciatore," he said, and then apologized for the state of the street.

"It should be paved, but the parish won't do it." He sighed. "We'll have to do it ourselves before next winter."

Now, a young man stepped out of the carriage, wide hat in hand. He bowed to the man. "Maestro Amati," he said, "buon pomeriggio."

"My son, David," the woman said simply.

They were brought to a large room where a fire burned in a blackened hearth that took up almost an entire side wall. They sat down at a table where a plate of sweet polenta, slices of capicola, and bitter greens awaited them with a jar of cooked wine.

"Per favore, help yourselves!" a woman said as she entered the room. "I am Lucrezia, Nicolò's wife. You've traveled far and must be starving. Please," she repeated, "Signora Cacciatore—"

"Call me Andréa," the traveler said.

"You are French, are you not?" asked Nicolò Amati, taking a slice of bread and bitter greens.

"I am, yes. I met Guilio, my husband, in Paris where he travels often for his trade. I joined him in London when we were married.

"Your Italian is eccellente," Lucrezia said.

"Better than David's," Andréa blushed, "but he understands well enough."

"He speaks French?" Nicolò asked.

"He does, perfectly. And English, naturally."

"E bene. I deal much with French and English envoys these days and their Italian is poor. He'll help, your son. We are now making a violin for the new young king Louis XIV. Ordered this last month by his mother, the reggente."

"Ann of Austria is a good mother, I hear," Andréa said. "Very attentive."

"You, signora, is good mother, too," Lucrezia said in

broken French. "You've come a long way to bring us your son. How old is he?"

"David is now five and ten years. I know your apprenticeship begins at a younger age, Maestro Amati, but I can assure you that ..."

"Age matters not." Turning toward the young man who was helping himself to more sweet polenta, he added, "Only the passion and the skills matter, yes, David?

"That is what my father says," the young man replied in broken Italian. "My father, he loves the music of the mandolin and he plays a little. I'd like to make one for him."

"You are a good son," Nicoló said.

"David has a special relationship with Guilio," Andréa said. "It broke Guilio's heart to see him leave, but he knows this is what David needs. David does not like the work of banking, and his father is good to understand that.

"I am told you have another son?"

"Sì, Adrian. He is already helping his father with banking. He is also the reason why I must return to London as soon as possible. He still needs his mother, my eldest," she added, blushing. "He..."

But she didn't explain further.

"Then, we must proceed," Nicoló said, standing up. "Please, signora, David, let me take you to my bottega."

The workshop was a very large, high-ceiling room located on the estate in an adjacent building. A strong scent of shaved wood, glue, and varnish permeated the air. The walls were lined with long, narrow clerestory windows through which abundant natural light poured over the formidable worktable in the center of the room. There were five wide cuts in the table where young men sat, working at different stages of fabrication. Alongside them were placed trays of tools: knives of all shapes, clamps, bending straps, blades, and tweezers, gouges, chisels.

David stood staring, fascinated.

All around them, on wide shelves going all the way to the windows, stood violins, lutes, violas, mandolins, guitars, and harps in all stages of assembly. Marveling, David went around, touching them all lightly with the tip of his fingers.

"May I have a word with you, maestro?" Andréa asked, after having walked around the room herself, observing keenly.

"Certo, signora," Nicoló answered, opening a side door and inviting her through.

The room was much smaller and a bit stuffy, but it held a couple of large, comfortable padded chairs and a small table with papers on it, obviously business correspondence.

Nicoló picked up a letter, and unfolded it, explaining, "These are words of recommendation I received from my friend Beppe in London."

"Guiseppe, you mean? Such a good, caring man. I met his wife when I first came to London, and she made moving there so much easier. She is also the one who teaches me your beautiful lingua."

"Guiseppe, we always called him Beppe. He was from Piacenza originally, did you know? Abandoned when his father remarried. A terrible situation until my grandfather took the boy in. He lived in this house with us, and I was his friend, although he was much older. When he left for England, we were all so desolate. We did not understand. But he is well, and that is all that matters."

"Very successful, too. A master builder for the crown. King Charles is quite trusting of him."

"That is very good, but monarchs die, and who knows with the next one who will be favored, and who will not!"

"Guiseppe is quite old, maestro. He is unlikely to outlive the king."

"Bene, bene. So, you want to tell me about David, I think? Beppe mentions that his mind is - let me see, and he looked down again at the letter in his hands. "Ah, sì, there it is. Beppe writes, 'David is a fine young man with a creative heart and disposition. But you should know that sometimes his mind is overtaken by what I can only describe as sweet madness. He is, for instance, wholly taken by the number five. He will work his jaw around bites of food five times before swallowing. He is discreet about it, and his physician believes it is just some kind of a youth fever that will stop with time. It would also seem that this repetition by five occurs only when he is frustrated and unable to focus his attention. That is why I believe that your workshop, caro amico, will help keep him secure and clearheaded. He does marvels when he draws.'"

"Yes, maestro, that is exactly what I meant to share with you. We noticed that when David is busy doing something he loves, such as drawing or carving, his mind is no longer feverish and the repetition stops."

"Cara, I have known in my time many good people

with strange personal - eh, how shall I put it - peculiarities. Yes, I believe that is what we should call it: peculiarities. We all have some, do we not? They cause no harm to anyone and are best ignored by others so as not to worsen them."

"Grazie, maestro. Thank you. Now if you'll allow me, I will take my leave. The way back home will be long and tedious, but I'll go with peace in my heart."

"Ma no, signora! You are with us less than half this day. You cannot take your leave without a proper stay. It would be folly!

"Be reassured, my dear Nicolò, that I am not going back to London all at once. Guilio has a cousin *en la nella de Lodi* who welcomed David and me for many days before we came to you. I will now return to him and his family before the long journey home. David knows how to go to them if needed. They are good people. And to reassure you further, know that I will also stop in France to see my own family."

"I am much comforted, signora, much comforted, but won't you want to see your son before being on your way?"

"No. We talked about it while in Lodi, and we both believe it is better for me to go without goodbye, so that we can both bear it."

"Capisco, signora, capisco. When do we hope to see you again?"

"I will return next spring, and for the time being, I will write. Both Guilio and I thank you much for the lodging. If you should need further settlement..."

"*Certo che no!* You have been most generous, signora, most generous. More than is needed for the boy to be kept well."

"Then what you wish might be achieved and that street of yours be paved?"

Signora Cacciatore smiled. "It will be done in your name, signora, for you to step out onto come spring."

NINE

Dylan?

Yes?

What do you think?

It's like one of your short stories. Different.

Different?

A bit out there.

Out there?

Look, I don't know what to say that you won't question. I like it, Ok? I like it because it's about me, and since there is nothing else anywhere for me, I'll take it. I mean, I loved living, Mom; I did, even when I hated my life.

I know, I know, and it's so hard to wrap my head around the fact that it only lasted twenty-three years and that out of these, only sixteen were truly free.

What's going to happen next? In Italy I mean.

Well, now that I have set things in motion, we have to give you time to get settled. The world then was a very slow one, in every sense of the word. Andréa, no doubt, will eventually get news from Cremona.

You will get news.

Yes, me in London. I quite like myself as Andréa. She is a good mother.

You are a good mother, Mom!

I am not bad. Rewriting myself, though, has its appeal! And Andréa is my middle name.

Will I have to brush my teeth? I mean, in Cremona? Did they brush their teeth back then in the slow world?

... ...

Why are you sighing?

Honestly, Dylan, what was the big deal about brushing your teeth?

Not my fault. I took after Mamie.

For real, now. Why was it such a drama each time I demanded that you go back to the bathroom and brush?

What do you think? How come you don't ever get it? I had to count, all right? I had to count and count again if I messed up. Same thing with walking. I had to count and watch every fucking step I made to avoid the cracks and lines on the sidewalk. I mean, it was insane!

I understand, and I apologize.

Okay.

Was there anything you didn't have to ritualize to?

My music when I really got into it. When I could get lost in it, I was all right.

I wouldn't call it *music...*

I can't believe you just said that. You thought it was trash, didn't you?

No! I wouldn't call it trash, no. It's just that...I'll explain. First, let me say that your brother did inform me that your beats were top-notch. Now, do I know what a beat is? No. What I know is that perhaps you shouldn't have put lyrics to it?

Jesus, Mom! Stop it with the mocking.

I am just saying.

No, you are not just saying. I know you. You are sneering at the only thing I truly loved, my music.

We had a deal. I said I wouldn't lie. I said I would tell the truth as I see it, as I feel it. And the truth is that I felt sad and angry and frustrated that all the talent you had shown since childhood in drawing, carving, and filmmaking went nowhere. That instead you lost yourself in a kind of music that is so foreign to my own personal sense of — of what? Beauty? Harmony? Yes, I confess, it's very partial, and cultural, and generational. I am sorry, Dylan, I don't mean to hurt you.

The only thing that's fucking hurting is that if you really thought about it, you would get why I was so much into music and no longer into drawing or movie-making.

Because of Boo?

There you go. See? That wasn't hard to grasp, was it? I got more and more into music because the thoughts kept getting louder, requiring more and more counting, more and more fucking rituals. With music blasting into my ears, I could get away from them, like almost, and when I was lucky, like totally. At the same time, I was into something I loved, and I loved my music just as Glenn loves his.

For him it's jazz and for me it was rap. Is that so hard to get into your head?

Again, I apologize. I can be such an idiot!

As you said, parents are the last to get it. It was what it was.

And will never be again. I wish I could have it all back, just the way it was.

No, you don't!
Dylan!

***

Mom?
Yes?
Tell me. If I had stuck around, do you think I could have made it? I mean, have a life?

In this world - here, today, I believe it would have been difficult. Way too busy, way too intense, and with too many communication tools to feed your obsessive mind. On top of that, society has become far too competitive and restrictive for someone like you.

Restrictive?

Restrictive in the sense that it mostly serves the technologically minded and the money-oriented ambitious. Even the creative mind has been hijacked to serve business and technology. It's all about conforming, and therefore much harder to survive for those who aren't wired that way.

And sure enough, I wasn't and I didn't.

But you could have. I am still convinced that had they let you run on the track team in high school, you would have lived well enough.

Oh, God! Talk about an obsessive mind! Listen to yourself going on and on about me and the stupid track team! I didn't even like running all that much. I knew I was good at it, but I did it mainly to do something, to make you happy.

No matter why you did it. You would have gotten hooked; that's what matters. You would have gotten hooked which in turn would have quenched your need for drugs, but you didn't get the chance. Your grades didn't improve, so they threw you off that team as well. What kind of twisted psychology is that? I mean, we are in the twenty-first century, for God's sake. Aren't we supposed to be way past basic ignorance?

The best remedy for troubled youths such as you is physical activity. Intense, regular physical activity. You don't need a PhD in psychology to know that. Educators, of all people, should know that! It's like preventing a restless five-year-old from going out to recess to teach him how to stand still! The absurdity of it!

Not to mention that they could have punished you in so many other ways, without having to deprive you of the only outlet to your restlessness. Actually, they should have ordered you on campus at six a.m. every morning to run. To run until you dropped. It would have saved you.

You don't know that. You don't know that and you don't know that I would have lived. So stop with the fixation and let's not speak about high school anymore, okay? It was too fucking humiliating.

You were not fit for a Catholic one; I see that now. Not to mention that it was too big to contain you, and you ran wild from day one. Academically it was way too rigorous, and religious studies...

Bored me!

...overwhelmed you. What a chorus we make!

So according to you, the Academy was too French and too rigid, and high school too Catholic and too rigorous. I needed a school designed just for me and my needs!

There was one, and we found it. It wasn't perfect, there was no running, but above all, it was too late. By then, Boo was in control.

...Only downers helped.

Downers you bought on the street with the money you stole from us. And enough of them to render you stupefied. You came home one day in such a lethargic state as to appear comatose. We thought you were having a psychotic breakdown! It was both scary and ugly to see you in that state.

That's mean, and you should know that being comatose is better than feeling like your mind is about to implode.

TEN

Dylan?

Yes?

I am sorry about what I said yesterday. I was unkind.

Seriously!

Last night I had a dream where I wrote you a poem. This morning I remembered it all and wrote it down without changing a word. Shall I read it to you?

Nope.

Why?

Just because.

Why?

Because it'll be sad and because you suck at poetry. That's why.

An unkind thing to say but you're right, I suck at poetry. You, on the other hand, wrote lovely poems.

Songs, Mom, I wrote songs.

That was later, with your music. I am talking about the time when you wrote old-fashioned poems. They were really good, Dylan. As for mine, I will keep it to myself since I can't possibly share it with Glenn and your brother.

Because they know you suck at poetry.

No. Because they always have a hard time going there.

Going where?

To you. They have both divided their hearts into little boxes and they have shut down the door to the one you inhabit. That's their way of coping with losing you and I respect that. It's a very masculine attribute I wish I had.

What attribute?

The ability to compartmentalize emotions. I can't. Most women can't. Our hearts can't be divided into little boxes. We only have the one with all emotions piled up inside. They are somehow wired together and shooting out every which way. It's quite exhausting but the one good thing is that my door to you is always wide open.

I am nowhere near any of Adrian's little boxes.

Of course, you are. Locked up, maybe even sealed off, but you are.

I am nowhere in his heart because he hates me.

No, he doesn't.

He did.

Oh, for God's sake Dylan, grow up!

There is no more growing up for me, Mom. Not where I am. And one thing I am fucking sure of is that Adrian doesn't miss me.

Not all of you, no. Then again neither do I, and neither does Glenn. We miss your boyhood and the generous, laughing you, but we do not miss the later you. From high school on, we stopped liking you because you were no longer likable. As youth began slipping from you, you became a stranger. Another you was taking over. It's like the Dylan we loved had only been a skin that a new, darker Dylan was shedding.

Like a snake.

Yes. I wish it was the darker Dylan alone who was gone. I wish he had left you behind.

Me, the dead skin. I won't grow old, Mom. I won't grow old and smelly and cranky, but Adrian will. He will grow old and smelly and cranky, and he won't miss me a minute. And don't say that he will. He never even liked me. Not ever.

It's not that he didn't like you. To begin with, there was the seven years' difference in age, which meant that you had different challenges, that you were not into the same things. There was also the fact that you had two very, very different personalities. Day and night, as they say.

The good son and the bad son.

Who is being melodramatic now? Your brother always had a hard time *getting* you; that's a given. As the years went by, it got harder for him to understand your behavior. Even when he caught up with the extent of your mental problems, he grew frustrated with your use of drugs, just as we did. On top of that, every time he came home, we were in some kind of a crisis, battling with you over drugs and money, and over the lies that went with it. The lies, Dylan! Adrian saw the damage they did, you understand? The sickness we could take ...

You couldn't.

Mea culpa, but no apologies. Living with your rituals was damn hard, and that last year was particularly taxing. You were now counting constantly. You even counted at the computer.

I was counting at the computer way before that last

year. Why do you think I quit art school, huh?

Because you stopped going to classes? Because you were wasted?

And why did I stop going to classes? Why was I wasted? Because most of our projects were done on the computer, that's why! Imagine having to tap three times on each of the fucking keys while writing or creating a project! Five times if I messed up!

I don't have to imagine. As I said, I saw you doing it at home.

You would leave the room!

Oh Dylan, I don't feel good about that. I don't feel good at all, but I couldn't help it, just like you couldn't help counting. You counted when you chewed, you even counted when you hugged me!

I could feel your whole body stiffen. I hated it.

And it got worse. It got worse when you began involving *me* in the counting.

I never did!

Yes, you did. I'd be in bed upstairs, and you'd call, "Goodnight, Mom" from down below. I would reply, "Goodnight, Dylan," and you'd call again "Goodnight, Mom" and I knew it would have to be repeated three times.

Oh, that.

Yes, that. What can I say? It now seems like something benign, something that surely could be indulged, but when it was happening, it was damn hard to go along with. It was like a flag being waved at me with OCD madness printed on it. Nothing felt spontaneous or natural anymore. What a mess we were!

You can say that again.

I can only apologize for not having been a saint about it, but even when I couldn't take the rituals, I understood the disorder. Of course, I bloody did! I saw Boo growing, one ritual at a time, one anxiety at a time and believe me, he left a long shadow every time he won the game. I saw him crushing each and every step we took to get you better. So, don't tell me I couldn't take the sickness. I did as much as I could. And I most certainly understood the craziness of it all. Again, what I couldn't take or understand were the lies. There came a time when we could no longer believe a word you said, Dylan.

It went with the sickness! I needed downers because only they stopped it from taking over my head. And to get the downers, I needed money. The fucking regular drugs the psychiatrist gave me didn't help. They didn't, you get that? Not since forever. Not the old ones and not the new ones from the new psychiatrist. Remember what I had to go through with the new one?

You went through hell. Hell because you had first to get off the med you had been taking for what - three, four years? - and the withdrawal was awful. It terrified me. I remember finding you outside on the patio in the middle of the night, tapping on the walls, banging your head on it. I understood then why, since you were medicated, you had to have a yearly ECG. The drugs you were taking could have weakened your heart.

Wasn't that great! And for nothing. For absolutely nothing since they didn't help.

They might have, had you taken them diligently. But you didn't. If dad or I didn't hand them to you and watch you take them, you forgot or chose not to take them. Probably because they didn't get you high.

There was that.

See?

What I see is that it proves my point. If they had worked, why would have I ever taken something else? Why the need to get high? On top of that, they made me sweat and feel nauseous. They messed up my stomach and my nights by giving me huge nightmares! On the other hand, with Xanax, I was feeling good like you couldn't believe!

I see.

Again, you don't. You don't see at all. As a normal person, when you don't feel good or sane it's nothing like when I didn't feel good and sane, which was pretty much all the time. So, to you, downers are just a messed-up drug. To me, they were my friends.

Oh! Dylan! What can I say?

Not a thing, Mom. There isn't a thing to be said.

Cremona, Lombardy, March 1648

Signora Andréa,

David has been with us almost ten months now, and I asked Signore Henry Greensbury, who is here painting, to write down my words since I myself write with great difficulty in Italian, and not at all in English.

We heard there is war among your good people and that you will be detained in London for many months to come.

Please trust that David is now better in health than he was last summer when he missed home so much we feared he would not heal.

To be sure, you know his affliction better than we, so you will understand that we were much anguished. He did not leave his bedchamber for many weeks and ate very little. We heard him pace and sometimes scream for you.

When we brought him to the bottega, the fever took over his spirit and made him greatly agitated. So much that he bruised his fingers knocking on the walls.

In the autumn, we called on your family in Lodi who arranged for Doctore Ludo Setta from Milan to come and see David. They spent many mornings together walking long and far, in all weather. The doctore gave him some herb potion mixed with *depalgos* which he tells us has great power to quiet all humors. The apothecary in Lodi sends more as needed.

David henceforth became less melancholy and after the good celebrations of Christmas, he came to the bottega, at peace with himself.

I assure you he is in good care with Nicolò, who believes only hard work can help his tired spirit. David bears the work with great patience.

He is a fine young man, your son. The other apprentices call him *cinque* since he favors that number and counts it many a time throughout the day. He touches his tools five times before using them, and pulls the door handles five times. And so, they call him *cinque* but he takes it in good humor since they mean no harm. Everyone is fond of David here.

Each day but that of the Lord, he spends six hours at work. He eats well and after supper, he studies the violin. Nicolò tells all his pupils that to build well you have to play well. He also tells me that your son has agile fingers and a sensitive ear.

We told David about the war at home, and he is most saddened that you won't journey back to us for the time being. He still cannot bear writing you himself for fear the fever will take over his spirit, but I don't doubt that this also will pass. We have to be patient.

I pray these words will find you in good health and spirit. They will be brought to you by Signore Greensbury with the painting you commissioned.

Affettuosamente,
Lucrezia

ELEVEN

After you dropped out of art school and moved back home you tried to work, but you couldn't keep a job more than a few days, a few weeks, a few months at Glenn's office because you were indulged there.

I tried, Mom, I really did! Everywhere I worked I tried. People just didn't like me or they didn't trust me. I don't know! Maybe they saw I was retarded?

You say that again and I'll …

You'll what? What can you do to me now?

I know you tried and I know how hard it was for you. I saw you struggle at that café on College Avenue. You were so proud you had found a job! I remember standing outside across the street and watching you carrying a tray, doing discreetly what you did with your feet, and...

Counting. I was counting my steps and I must have looked what I was, a weirdo. I also had to move empty coffee cups a few times before picking them up to put them on the fucking tray. I wasn't even a waiter; I was a busboy! I was a fucking busboy who couldn't even do his job! It was worse at Glenn's office because I really wanted to do well, and I really wanted to like it, and I tried my hardest but I just couldn't get into whatever it was I was asked to do.

Oh, I know. I know you tried. Dad's assistant told me. We had lunch together one day, and I asked how you were doing. She hesitated, and I could see the question made her uncomfortable, so I told her to just tell me like it was. She thought about it for a minute before saying, "He reminds me of a bird trapped in a cage, flapping its wings uselessly at all corners."

And then she added, "He tries to be discreet about his rituals, but I can see that they are increasing, and it's heartbreaking."

***

You got deeper into opioids, deeper into your lies, and the tension at home kept rising. When you weren't looking for a job, you slept all day and went out at night to find drugs and company. Drugs to not be alone with your head and company to not be alone with drugs. I was always on edge, worrying, wondering where you were, what you were doing, and with whom. What kind of trouble were you getting into?

When you were around, we screamed at each other. We screamed and cried, screamed and cried, and I'd storm out of the room and then it would be you and Glenn screaming. Because unlike me, you never walked out on us. You always wanted to explain, to justify, to talk it out, even when we had enough, even when we just wanted you out of sight. You insisted in explaining yourself because even while lying, you wanted our approval. It was such a genuine, such an anguished need on your part that it made it impossible for us to deny you.

I felt like such a fucking failure. You know that, don't you?

I do and I did, but it was still hard to live through it day after day. At times, mostly at night, it was so overwhelming that I was the one to get out. I'd go and drive around aimlessly before parking my car somewhere to stare at the dashboard, at the sky across the windshield, at the bay, at the trees, at my hands, at anything just to remain sane.

Mom, stop. It hurts!

Everything went crashing down in the spring when you were arrested in the middle of the night with two friends in a parking lot in Berkeley. One of them had a small bag of weed with him, and the other some cocaine. Cops in Berkeley were pretty indulgent when it came to pot and coke for personal consumption, but they arrested you because you provoked them by opening your big mouth and emptying your jeans pockets. Three oxycodone pills fell onto the ground, and you were cuffed then and there.

You'd been arrested twice before, but since you were a minor, they hadn't taken you to jail. Instead the police had brought you home or had come knocking for us to go pick you up at the station. You went to court both times, for misdemeanor offenses. The first time because one afternoon after school, in a park near home, you brandished a Swiss Army knife at kids you claimed were bullies.

They were, Mom, they totally were, white kids screaming racist slurs at my friend!

You pulled out a knife in front of a cop off duty, Dylan!

Yeah, me and my good luck! What was he doing there anyway?

And what were you doing with a knife in your pocket?

I don't remember. Found it?

How about stole it?

No! Why do you always think the worse of me?

Why? Perhaps because the second time you were arrested, you had stolen two twenty-dollar bills from the cash register of the local video store, right under the security camera! Forty dollars, Dylan! How stupidly juvenile was that?

I was fifteen, Mom. I was fifteen, and my friend was working there. Stealing forty dollars was just a dare. A joke.

Stealing money is never a joke, not to mention that you did it just before going to court for the knife story! I thought I would lose my mind.

The judge ordered you to do three hundred hours of community service. You did it on weekends for six months, in one of the city animal shelters. Of course, you loved it there! To me, it felt more like a reward for your foolishness than a punishment to learn from.

This time - the third time, since you were now of age, they sent you to Santa Rita county jail. You called us at three thirty in the morning and...

You hung up on me!

Because you were high and hysterical. Because when you said you had been arrested for drug possession, I didn't want to hear. I wanted to scream. So yes, I hung up. I hung up thinking that this time you would have to learn your lesson. I hung up thinking that a few days in Santa Rita would clear your head and give you a much-needed reality check. But you called right back, and your father picked up.

I was terrified! I spent three nights there with real criminals in a single room with benches bolted to the walls to sit on, a roll of toilet paper to lay my head on, and one urinal in the corner! One urinal for eleven guys. It was horrible. The guards kept laughing at us and telling us the wrong time so we never knew what time of day or night it was. Actually, when someone asked, they always gave the same answer: They'd say, it's three o'clock, man. As for the assholes in there with me, some kept staring, egging me on about why I was there. Was I a working boy? That's what they thought, Mom! And you know what they do to working boys? To white working boys? To boys period?

All this because of three pills I had for my own needs! I wasn't selling, I wasn't hurting anyone but me, was I? So why send me to this hell hole with pimps and drug dealers? Wasn't it a bit disproportionate?"

Of course, it bloody was disproportionate. And ridiculous and unfair, but there you go. You do something illegal; you pay whatever price they set. You should have known better.

We had to hire a criminal lawyer. He got you out but you were ordered to enter a rehab program for eight months and to visit the probation office every week for a urine test. Early December, the day after your last urine test, you went back to the drugs, and at home the dynamics tilted back into darkness.

Those were the hardest months of all my years.

I found myself trapped in an endless spin of raw emotions - anger, resentment, love, dismay, fear. I knew, at a certain level and without ever articulating it, not even to myself - as if keeping it quiet would contain the inevitable - that you were lost, caught in a web of disorders that were inexorably overtaking you. Had you only suffered from dyslexia, it would have been all right. Had you only suffered from ADD, or from OCD, it would have been all right. The three together were a fight we could not win.

Comorbidity is the medical word, and it implies interactions between the disorders that can worsen the course of them all. In your case, it brought paralyzing anxieties, and your rituals increased proportionally to your need for escape into a state of senselessness. A state that only downers could provide.

That year of 2013, your panic attacks escalated. You'd call me from the bus stop to tell me you couldn't move. On the phone, I'd help you control the waves of panic by making you bend your head down between your legs, telling you to breathe in, to breathe out, to breathe in and out deeply, slowly, repeatedly.

The vision of the tall, gray-eyed woman in the parking lot of a supermarket wasn't helping anymore. I knew that no crowd, not ever, would cheer you.

We still laughed together, though, didn't we? We did, Mom, even that last year. I loved how we laughed.

It felt like stepping into a pocket of time out of time. A warm and safe pocket, a pocket where nothing could hurt us. A pocket where Boo couldn't get in. You'd come to my bedroom and lie down next to me, asking me to scratch your back, and I'd ask you to mimic people. You'd do your old teachers, your old classmates, your favorite TV show characters! You were hilarious.

And you would do Mamie recounting the crazy situations she found herself in. Like the night she took a hitchhiker in her old 2-Chevaux, in the middle of nowhere, only to find out he was bad news.

I don't know about bad news - he probably was no longer dangerous - but unnerving, to be sure! He'd asked her to drop him at the next village church rectory where he was to meet with the vicar, and she was curious. He didn't look like a church person. He didn't look like the religious type at all. She asked him where he came from and when he said he'd gotten out of prison that very morning after spending twenty years in, she went mum. You don't ask a guy what he did to get a twenty.

So funny! Only Mamie would get into that kind of situation.

Which was good since it made for good stories that kept us laughing. In these moments, tucked with you in our little pocket out of time, I believed that if we went on laughing, nothing harmful and irrevocable could ever happen to us. Our laughs would keep the darkness at bay. The darkness and the nightmares.

I hated my nightmares.

Who doesn't hate nightmares? Did I tell you about the one I had after I last saw you? About a tsunami coming in from across the mountains?

You didn't, and I don't remember when I saw you last. When was it?

You came home that Sunday afternoon to make copies of your résumé. By Tuesday night you were gone, and the very last image I have of you is at the front gate. I am standing way up the path behind you, and you are doing with your feet what you always did when you were stressed: Tap tap tap - three times before pulling the gate open, tap tap tap - three times after closing it behind you without looking back. You didn't look back, and I didn't call you back. I write that, I write that I didn't call you back, and tears come flowing down my face. It's a terrible thing, the fact that I didn't call you back. It's a fact I'll have to bear the rest of my life. How can I?

It wouldn't have changed a thing, Mom. Just postponed the fall, as you would say.

We don't know that. And now, we'll never know.

Tell me about the tsunami.

The tsunami? Ah, yes, my nightmare. In it, I am looking out my window at a range of mountains, dark and ghostly, knowing in my guts that a tsunami is fast approaching. I go around the house, frantically searching for my passport so I can get to the airport and fly away before the cataclysm reaches me.

I woke up drenched in sweat and screaming. The bedroom was quiet, neither Manouche at the foot of the bed, nor Lili stretched out behind my head, nor Glenn at my side had stirred. I had been screaming silently.

That's a sick dream, Mom.

And so ominous I still can't take it all in.

***

Mom?
Yes?
Are you all right?

I'll live, but no, I am not all right. Of course, I am not all right. How could I be all right? I am still raw with pain and anger. Anger at your carelessness, anger at Boo. As for the pain, it's here twenty-four/seven. Sometimes at night in the pit of my dreams it pulls at me with such intensity that I have to force myself awake so as not to drown in my own sorrow.

How about Glenn? Is he all right?

Your dad, too, gets overwhelmed with grief.

I thought you said he had locked me up in a little box and thrown away the key.

I never said he threw away the key and, in any case,, you come bursting through the box now and then, and nothing can stop you. The fact that he has been working at the piano on a song for you, *Dylan Blues,* doesn't help keeping you in. One evening he tried to sing it out loud to me, but he kept choking on his own lyrics and I had to hold him tight for the pain to recede. Since then he plays the tune on his sax or at the piano, but the lyrics remain tucked away in a drawer.

Stop. I am feeling so bad right now!

Okay, let's stop here. I am not feeling so good either.

***

Dylan?

Mmmmmumh

Are you still upset?

About fucking up your life? What do you think?

How about your brother? You still believe he hated you?

Yeah, I do. When I came back from Mexico, he even

said he wished I was dead. Actually, he didn't say it, he yelled it.

Bad choice of words, but we all said terrible things when you acted stupid and deceptive, which was pretty much all the time those last few years. Did you lie to your shrink, too?

Not at the beginning. I tried to keep it straight for a long time, but then, when I realized that seeing him didn't make any difference, I pretty much told him what he wanted to hear, although when I said it, I believed it. In that room with him, I believed I could control whatever was going on in my head. I believed I could stop taking pills. I didn't even feel like I was sick. He couldn't help me, Mom, nobody could and he didn't see that, but he was nice.

We didn't pay him to be nice!

There you go. As for Adrian, he was the one to suggest Mexico, and I hated him for that. You all knew I didn't want to go. And weren't you the one who always said that when you do something you don't want to do, when you do something because you are forced to or only to please someone, like going to therapy, it doesn't work? I just went for you and Glenn. I just went for you guys, not for me.

Oh, Dylan, what can I say? You are right. Forcing someone to do something he is unwilling to do leads often to failure.

You said "always."

We were desperate, don't you see? With no more options to consider, it was like facing an insurmountable wall. Do you dig a hole under it large enough to crawl through and risk having the entire structure collapse, or do you just give up and wait for the inevitable? The inevitable being that one of us would seriously lose it...

That would be you.

...or you would overdose.

Which I did.

Because you came back! Because you didn't even try to make it work! Adrian had worked very hard to find that organization of volunteers where you were to teach art to fatherless children. It wasn't forced labor, for crying out loud, or the army, was it? Honestly, what could have been better? You loved art, you loved children, and the town of San Miguel is peopled with artists and expats. It was a wonderful opportunity, and you blew it. You just bloody blew it. Come on, say it. Say, I blew it.

I blew it.

You signed up for six months, and...

No. No, Mom, I didn't sign up for anything. You signed me up for six months.

And you were sacked after a week. *One week*, Dylan. How do you think that made us feel? Yes, Adrian was furious! Still, he talked on Skype for over an hour with the head of the organization there to try to fix things. She told him that the kids adored you, that you obviously were a gifted instructor, but for God's sake, Dylan, you stayed out all night and fell asleep in class with the kids, practically upon arrival. You found drugs there, didn't you?

Not true! I was just drinking Tequila and staying up too late.

Oh, excuse me! You were just drinking tequila and staying up too late! And you think that makes it better?

Don't blame your brother for being furious. Of course, he was furious. I was furious, too, and so was Glenn. You weren't there three days when you called to tell us you had lost the two hundred dollars in cash you had left with! Or it had been stolen, you weren't sure. And your father believed you! He actually believed you! I was screaming! In fact, what you did with the money, along with paying for the tequila, was spend it on a new tattoo inked across your right hip!

How do you know about that?

It was on the autopsy report. You just couldn't stop lying, that's what! Lying and indulging yourself in any way you could, with not a thought about how it affected us.

That's not true!

Well, it bloody felt like that to me, and no wonder everything went downhill from there! You came back after a week, and what did you do the following night? You went out and did drugs again.

No, I didn't.

Because you didn't find any, if I remember correctly! And as if that wasn't enough, you went out with that schizophrenic young man you knew and who, when he got back home in the early hours of that awful morning, tried to kill his parents! They had to call the cops, for heaven's sake! What were you thinking? Didn't it occur to you that by surrounding yourself with drug dealers and a seriously mentally ill young man who could have turned on you, you were putting us all in danger?

I had just failed you in Mexico, I knew you hated my guts, and I couldn't stand myself. I actually wanted to die that night.

Ah, Jesus! Stop it with the we hated you. As if it were that simple. Sure, we didn't like you, and how could we? You had painted the three of us in a corner from where we felt helpless, angry, and scared. Hard truth that, isn't it? What were your father and I supposed to do? What was your brother supposed to do or say? He felt defeated and he felt betrayed. That's how he felt. You had left us all at a complete loss.

... ...

Dylan?

... ...

Dylan?

Enough for now, Mom, please? Let me go back to nowhere for a while, okay?

Cremona, Lombardy, July in the year 1652

Cara Andréa,

Your letter was well received, and we are heartened to hear that you are in good health. Ambrose Warwick, a gentleman from Oxford town, here to purchase a violin for the Earl of Oxford, tells us that the commonwealth of your Lord Cromwell is fighting itself. We pray you will be spared a fourth war.

Sir Ambrose is writing my words down in English, and he will bring them to you when he stops in London, on his way back to Oxford town.

I have good news, cara Andréa, I am with child! Nicolò is so joyous and confident it is a lad, I fear his heart will shatter if a baby girl comes!

Another good news is that your David is in love! He cannot wait for you to meet his betrothed Alessandra. I do not doubt that you will love her as a daughter. She is from a good family of cabinetmakers who live five dwellings from us. David has known her and her three brothers since you brought him here five years past, and to be sure, he was always taken by her amber eyes and her vivacity. She is two years and three months older than he is, and tells me she was also besotted at first sight! David is most kind to her, and her family holds him in great esteem.

She is a fine embroideress, Alessandra, and much in demand for her cloth among noble women, as far as Milan. Her embossed work on cabinets is also much praised as her intricate decorative stitches are sui generis. She cares deeply for your son and helps quiet his spirit whenever his affliction rises. I am sad to say that the fever still takes hold of him, and he can get quite distressed if the potion Dottore Ludo Setta advised him to take is late coming from Lodi. He gets fast tormented then, with much sweat and shivers, and violent shaking of his hands.

David and Alessandra will become man and wife in the autumn, and will leave for Paris in spring. David plans to open his own workshop there. He is much talented with the making of bows, your son, and he carves their heads with a fine touch.

I doubt not that Alessandra herself will quickly be known for her cloth amongst the good ladies of Paris.

I pray you keep well in health and spirit.

Affettuosamente,

Lucrezia.

TWELVE

Tuesday, April 29, 2014

They came at around ten p.m. on the last Tuesday of April. There were two of them. A man and a woman. When Glenn saw them walk up the driveway in the harsh glow of the motion light, he thought, "What did he do now?"

The woman asked him if he was Glenn Hunter, and he said, "Yes, I am Glenn Hunter." She asked if he was Dylan Hunter's father, and he said, "Yes, I am, what is this about?"

The man told him that earlier that evening, you had been found dead in an apartment in the depths of West Oakland. Your body had been removed and was now at the coroner's office. There would be an autopsy the following day. A week later, the toxicology report would tell us that you'd died of an overdose of methadone and diazepam. You were twenty-three years old.

I didn't mean to die, Mom, I swear I didn't. I'd never have done that to you. It's just that I was feeling so bad that night. I had gone out to eat some crap with the friends I stayed with, and when we got back — I don't know. They went to sleep because they had to leave early in the morning for art school in the city.

That's where you'd met them.

Yes, in animation class. They lived in a dump on the fourth floor of a bigger dump because they couldn't afford anything better. Black kids from Texas they were, on scholarship. West Oakland was the only option although they couldn't really do any work there since there was no access to the internet. There was no bathroom either. Just one toilet in the corridor on each floor. Filthy. They had let me come over, but there wasn't much room. That night I went in the closet that was my bedroom and lay down on my air mattress that had no air left. Remember how hot it was?

Yes. It was stifling.

I couldn't even open the tiny window because it was stuck shut.

I know. The following day Adrian and I went there to get your belongings. The cops had given Glenn the address and your friend Aaron's phone number. He and his girlfriend were devastated. Absolutely devastated.

I asked them to open the window so that your soul - Your spirit? Your energy? -the immaterial part of you could fly away. It's an old Danish tradition that always spoke to me because whatever your beliefs or disbeliefs about the other side of life, thinking that the very essence of someone you love can be released and set free is comforting. It's like a promise of deliverance. It's letting go, and it's also letting in - a new day, a new tomorrow.

Aaron, of course, knew that the window was stuck, so he wrapped his fist in his t-shirt and broke it.

On the floor, near the airless mattress, there was the

stain of your vomit.

I told Aaron I would pay to fix the window, but he said no, everything in this building is so squalid that all the windows should be smashed to let some air in. His girlfriend said, "The air outside isn't much better."

What Aaron wanted from me was a translation of "Pater Noster," the French poem tattooed on your chest just above the heart. He'd seen it when he tried to resuscitate you.

Notre Père qui êtes aux cieux,
Restez-y,
Et nous nous resterons sur la terre,
Qui est parfois si jolie.

You had seen it taped above my desk all your life and you had it tattooed because you loved it.

No, Mom. I had it tattooed because I loved you.

I translated it — *Our Father in heaven, Stay there, And we'll stay here on earth, Which is sometimes so pretty* — but Aaron wanted it in French, so I wrote it down in French. Eventually, he too would have it tattooed on his chest.

Aaron is a good guy. That night I should have gone to him, but I didn't have the strength. It was so damn hot, so depressing. I mean, it was the pit and I was in it, and I knew I couldn't get out of it. I took some diazepam to go to sleep, but I slept like hell. I kept having these fucking dreams and a headache the size of I don't know what. In the early morning, I finally fell into my own pit of sleep. No dreams.

When I woke up in the middle of the afternoon, my head was swimming, and I felt like shit. It was hotter than ever, and I couldn't even get out of there since I didn't have the key to the building to get back in. On top of that, someone had stolen the seat of my bicycle that was chained to the gate. The seat, Mom! They'd steal anything in the depth of Oakland. Anything. Even the fucking seat of a fucking bicycle. I took more pills.

With the methadone you had gotten on the street.

Yeah. I fronted it. Not a good idea, I know.

And a bloody dangerous one. These guys would have come after you with a baseball bat, once they'd realized you weren't about to pay. Meanwhile, we thought that having no money would prevent you from buying drugs! How naive we were! But never mind that. A worse idea was for you to mix diazepam and methadone. For crying out loud, Dylan, you Google it and it's written as clear as tears: deadly combination.

Yeah. Sent me straight off to nowhere land. I should have known better. I actually knew better, but I didn't care. It was time for me to go, even though "me" didn't really decide it. Me was too high!

What a terrible thing to say, sweetie.

Terrible, but true, obviously. And you know what? I just fell asleep feeling high and good. Real good like, and I am not making this up.

Oh, I believe you. It's like overdosing on morphine. You don't feel yourself go. You fall asleep, you stop breathing - just like that. I know because ten years or so ago, I was in hospital for an emergency appendix surgery. It was serious enough to fear peritonitis. It went well, but afterwards the pain was so awful that I begged the nurse to give me something stronger than whatever it was I had been taking. She injected me with morphine.

A solid dose, I suspect.

A while later two friends came to visit. Nicola, a doctor, was one of them. I got up to go pee and began falling asleep on the toilet seat. I hadn't told them I was loaded with morphine, but Nicola thought as much and within minutes she came to check on me in the bathroom. I was barely breathing, falling asleep, about to slip away.

And you are telling me that now because?

Because I will always remember how I felt, sitting on the hospital loo. I felt heavenly. I felt so good and so far away from myself that I didn't want to leave that state. The quiet euphoria lasted until Nicola shook me to a stand-up position and slapped my face, forcing me to walk. She saved my life.

That's why I know you didn't suffer. That's why I know you fell asleep not only feeling good but blissful. I saw it on your face when Glenn and I came to say goodbye at the funeral parlor, in that beautiful room that looked like a chapel. Because there had been an autopsy you were wrapped up like a mummy, your head on top was misshaped under the bandages, as if they had rushed to put it back together. Your face untouched and serene, and there was a faint smile on your lips. I knew that smile. And what both relieved and overwhelmed me was realizing that in that peacefulness there wasn't a trace of Boo left.

***

That Tuesday afternoon, and perhaps at the exact time you left for the unknown, I badly twisted my ankle on the driveway. I wasn't rushing out, I didn't slip or stumble, I was only walking. I was only walking and my foot suddenly buckled under me. Thinking about it now, my mind strays a bit into the possibility of precognition.

That evening, I went to bed early.

The next thing I knew, Glenn was shaking me awake, crying out that you were gone.

Gone?

There are words that one simply can't speak. Or write. I haven't written it yet, and probably never will. You were gone, that's it. We called Adrian home from San Francisco, and the three of us sat, stood, paced, sat back down, stunned and shaken. We said little, we said what one says in time of tragedy, when not knowing what to say.

Glenn: He is at peace now.

Me: He needed to sleep.

Adrian: I feel so bad. I told him I wanted him to die.

Glenn: Those damned drugs ...

Adrian: Damn you, Dylan!

Me: It was inevitable.

That you had gone to sleep forever wasn't a surprise to any of us. Sleep was always the safest place for your tormented mind. At a certain level, it almost made sense your leaving it all.

We sat there wondering, but not devastated.

The devastation of having a son, a brother with growing psychological problems had already happened. We were something else, too. Something hard to admit, but there you go. We were relieved.

Relieved? Mom, that's kind of mean.

141

But true. We were relieved because the fear, the anger, the cries, the worries and toxicity of the previous seven years or so were, all at once, gone. I would no longer have to stand still with fear every time I heard police sirens in our street, every time the phone rang, every time there was a knock on the door.

All of the agony was gone, but it left me exhausted.

Sometimes I wondered if things would have turned out differently had we not, upon your return from Mexico thirteen days earlier, told you that you could no longer live at home. That we would be putting you in an assisted living home for young adults.

No way I could have ever done that, Mom. I was OCD, not lunatic!

I understand how humiliating it felt, but what else could we do to keep you safe away from home? It didn't happen, anyway. You left the next day to go live farther north in suburbia, with a friend we'd never met, a friend who'd agreed to give you room and board for five hundred dollars a month. Since he was himself a recovering addict, his only condition was that you would not do any drugs. What could we do? We agreed to the deal, and you left with a check.

"Mom, don't worry, I'll be all right," you said, and you wanted to hug me, but I didn't let you. You tried, but I turned away. I turned away and thirteen days later you had left this world. How am I ever going to forgive myself?

I forgive you, Mom.

Of course, you do. You were always so much better than me at forgiving. I hold grudges; you never did.

Are you kidding me? Of course, I did. Serious ones,

too! Against many people. Against that friend I gave the check for five hundred dollars to, and who still threw me out of his apartment three days later.

He threw you out because he found Xanax in your bag.

He had no right to search my bag!

Don't play indignant with me, Dylan. You had no qualms sneaking around the house to find money. In any case, your good friend threw you out, and you were so desperate that you called a girl from high school you never cared about and hadn't seen in four years!

I had taken her to the prom! She was in love with me.

Oh, that explains it. How clever of you! I actually remember her quite well. She was a lovely girl with a very fragile psyche. She picked you up in her car and took you home to her parents with whom she still lived in Alameda. You had hoped you could stay there. "We were thinking about it," her father told us when Glenn and I went to retrieve the few things you had left behind — your keyboard, clothes that had been washed and folded — "but our daughter is still terribly vulnerable, her mental health isn't... and... well..." He couldn't finish the sentence.

"What a nice boy Dylan was!" the mother said. "He made a vinaigrette for us the evening he stayed for supper. He even wrote down the recipe for me!"

The sweet you, the sweet you till the end.

THIRTEEN

Today, I am still more overwhelmed by the quiet you left behind than by your absence. My emotions are still all tied up in a cluster of a thousand knots. I didn't mourn you for the longest time because I had, or so I thought, already done all the mourning I could, and then some. I believed I had gone through all the stages of losing you while you were still around: denial, anger, hopelessness, fear, and hard, crushing sorrow.

Now that Boo is gone, now that I am left with what I choose to remember and to hold on to — the tender you, the generous you, I realize that I am far from having done my mourning. I look at the drawings you did in middle school, all incredibly detailed and beautiful, and I weep. I close my eyes and see you in the kitchen filming little stories with foil and string, ketchup, and charcoal, and I weep. Do you remember the last short film you made?

Of course, I do. It was at the art school and you had written the script.

From an old short story of mine, and because you hadn't come up with anything yourself! As usual you were late, and you'd asked me to help. And as always, the idiot that I was did.

Dylan Hunter's short film project: *The Impostor*

While vacationing in France, a young American man meets a young French woman. They have a fling and when he returns home, they pursue a romance through correspondence. Months later he receives a call from her. She is in San Francisco. He tells her that he'll meet her downtown in front of a café on Sutter Street.

He shows up and spots her immediately, farther up on the other side of the busy street. He waves his hands, but she doesn't see him. As he starts running up the street, he is shocked to see himself - another he? a duplicate? a clone? - exiting the café. The young woman throws herself into his arms.

Unbelieving, the young man dashes across the street, only to be run over by a car. As people rush and gather around his body, the imposter walks calmly back to the scene and grabs his backpack, which had been thrown onto the pavement. He then walks back to the unaware young woman. The last shot is of his face as he looks back over his shoulder to stare into the camera.

The script reads: Look like you are not from here. Like you come from another planet.

Very Twilight Zone this idea of being overtaken by another self.

And ominous since I had written the story when you were still whole, when Boo was still dormant.

Shooting the scene of the car running me over wasn't

easy.

Again, Dylan, it was a last-minute job, a rushed job, and as a result, a botched job. The film was pretty bad.

My head was not in it, and how could have I been motivated? I wasn't good at anything at the institute. The first year I sucked at drawing, and the second year I sucked at animation.

Only because you didn't apply yourself.

It wasn't that, and you know it. We've been there, so stop insulting me.

I didn't mean to. Let's take a break again. I am beginning to feel sick.

***

You had "Pater Noster" tattooed in French on your chest and you had *Hunter* tattooed on one shoulder. On the other shoulder, you had the *croix occitane* below the word *Languedoc.* You had seen this cross since childhood in the south of France, and you had seen it as a sticker on the back of my car.

I always liked it.

It's the symbol of the land I come from. A tough land. A rebellious land. So rebellious that in the Middle Ages the Pope launched a crusade against its people. He wanted to eradicate a powerful spiritual revival that had swept across the land, and that stood against the corruption of the Catholic...

Enough, Mom! Enough with history. You just can't stop, can you? I liked the cross, I liked its design, and I liked the fact that it represented where you grew up. That's all. How are things at home? How is Mamie?

Mamie is sorry to still be here on earth while you are not. She says, "C'est pas normal, c'est pas dans l'ordre des choses." It's not normal, it's not in the order of things. I tell her, "There is no order, Maman, and 'normal' is just a word."

She shakes her head sadly and says, "He should have been raised in the Fifties in France, at home in the south. He would have been sheltered there, out of harm's way. Like your aunt, he would have been considered a bit odd...

more like retarded...

...but there would have been no drug to mess him up. And in the countryside, in some isolated farms, there were still many old women with healing powers. I knew a few."

Not again! Not another life in another time with witches, please!

They were not witches, Dylan. They were women who, living so close to nature and the primitive world, had acquired a solid knowledge of the invisible and of the possible. Not to mention knowledge of medicinal herbs, fungi, and spices.

In any case, I am not sure about that world for you. Yes, it was a good place for children to grow up in, and probably still is. Lots of freedom because the immediate world around was so safe. But the Sixties and their road to drugs would have been too close for comfort.

And you said that there was no TV. That must have sucked.

Things don't suck, Dylan, when you never had them. Things don't suck when you don't even know what they are. I was nine years old when we got our first one in

1961. A black and white with one channel, and no program for teens. A few for children on Wednesday afternoons between one and four p.m.

No school on Wednesday afternoons, then?

No school on Wednesday afternoons.

But French teachers. French teachers like Monsieur, full of themselves and teaching an ultra-rigid curriculum.

There was that. The downside of an otherwise gentle and unhurried world. A more wholesome world where, to communicate, you actually had to talk to a person face to face. When I wanted to see a friend, I had to walk over to her house. In a small town of eight thousand people such as mine, residents didn't have a phone.

Another thing that must have totally sucked.

Again, when you don't know any better, you don't think your world sucks, as you put it. In my town, there were phones where they were needed; the doctor had one to be connected to the pharmacist and to the hospital, the hospital had one to be connected to the doctor and to the pharmacist, the bank had one to be connected to other banks, a few shops, such as my dad's, had one to be connected to suppliers, the police station and the mayor's office had one, the PG&E guy on call had one, and that was that. But it was a world free of drugs and, more importantly, it was a world where working a trade was honorable.

Not for Mamie!

Not for her daughter, no. But that was later, in the Sixties. I am talking about the years after the war. After the war and throughout the Fifties, good craftsmanship was in high demand at all levels of daily life. You could have trained as a cabinetmaker, as an upholsterer, as a leather artisan or, better still as a restorer. Restoring was your grandfather's passion and your grandfather was a very skilled craftsman. You took after him.

I remember the double-deck hut he made for Miss Rosie. It was really cool! I stood there while he did it, handing him tools and nails and he really worked at it to make it pretty!

He had trained as a cabinetmaker, although his talents went far beyond that. Had he had a choice, he would have been a professional restorer.

Why didn't he?

It's a long story.

Like I don't have all the time in the world?

I am not writing about my father, Dylan. I am writing about you and what's relevant to you. It's not a good idea to stray.

Who says?

Well, to begin with, the rules of writing a memoir.

Do these rules include the make believe of a life in seventeenth century Italy? Of conversing with the one that slipped away? And when did you ever follow a rule, Mom? Not to mention that it's my grandfather we're talking about, so how is that not relevant to me?

Oh, all right, it's lineage after all! On to my father then, for a short while.

Way before I came along, my father worked for the family upholstery and leather business. For extra money, he also spent his weekends at his uncle's workshop where he had already learned, after school throughout his youth, the skills to restore furniture.

Working for his father had never been his choice. As

a youngster, he had another vision of what his life could be - that of an engineer. That vision was cut down in 1945 after the war when his father ordered him out of school to help with the family business. He was sixteen years old and very bright. In fact, he was so good at math and science...

He sure didn't pass that on to you and me!

...that the headmaster begged my grandfather to let him finish high school. The old man wouldn't hear of it. He needed my father at the shop and that was that.

Six years later and soon after marrying Mamie...

Wait. You're saying that Papi got married at twenty-two?

He did. It was quite the average age to get married at the time. Mamie was twenty-six, practically a spinster. In any case, he had just gotten married and was at long last about to leave the family business and move to Paris to work as a restorer. A wealthy antiques dealer, who had many times visited my great uncle's workshop and seen my father's work, had offered to set him up.

The dealer had a space attached to his store, and he would handle both the moving and the finances. "Just get ready to work," my father remembered him saying. "Your hands will make you gold."

It was not to be. My grandfather fell ill, and within weeks he was dying. At his deathbed, he called not his eldest son, whom he loathed, but my father. He made him promise to stay to run the family business and raise his younger siblings.

What could my father do? There were three younger siblings. He stayed.

That sucks!

He didn't give up his passion altogether, though. I was very young, but I clearly remember the atelier he kept at home, where he spent his evenings working on ancient wardrobes, armchairs and the like while listening to the little transistor radio sitting on his workbench. Then one day the room was cleared out, and one of its walls broken down to enlarge the living room.

"Why?" I demanded to know years later. "You loved restoring!"

It was 1979, and I was home to announce that I would be leaving for the United States in the coming summer. We had drifted into memory lane, talking about my childhood, the house, my own recollection of events. "You loved restoring period pieces, and you stopped just to enlarge the living room?"

"No, it wasn't that," he explained, although that explanation didn't quite ring true to me. "Times were changing. My brother and I had given up the side of the business that dealt with making leather goods for horses and carriages, to replace it with carpet laying, which was the new big thing in homes in the late Fifties. I had no more time for restoring."

That sucks, too!

Doesn't it! Carpet laying for a man with such talent! What a waste. He just did what he had to do, I guess, what he thought was better for the family. That's what his generation did — what they had to do. He had a great sense of duty, my father, and a great sense of order. My goodness, his sense of order! Borderline OCD if you ask me.

Really? How come?

Being a builder, he had a huge collection of tools,

dozens of them of all shapes and sizes displayed in the garage. Each one was assigned a spot on the wall, marked with its own drawing above a hook. And each was hung just so, not one millimeter this way or that. He called it his great sense of order and precision.

But you think it was OCD?

His sister was, so it would make sense. With him, though, it was just a tendency.

Did he ever make something for you?

What do you mean?

Build something special like?

No, not really. I mean, nothing artsy if that's what you mean. But I remember the little pink wooden chair he made for me. I was, what, two, three years old? About that age, but I remember it very clearly. It had a rounded back that wrapped around my sides and four little feet that looked like actual paws.

I remember sitting happily on it in the cramped kitchen of the tiny one-bedroom apartment we lived in before we moved into our own house on the outskirts of town. I was not yet four years old when we moved into that house, so you see, I am not far off when I say I was about two or three at the time of the pink wooden chair.

The apartment was located above an auto-repair shop at the entrance to a very narrow street. In fact, it was so narrow that Mamie and the woman living at the same level across the street had stretched out a clothesline between their windows. "Not that there was any sun," Mamie told me, "but it was better than trying to dry the laundry inside, especially with the odors of oil and grease that came up from the shop below and permeated everything."

That feels so much like another world, Mom!

It was another world. I sat on the little chair in front of what was, to my two-year-old eyes, a gigantic stove. My head barely reached the middle of the oven door, and I could almost place my feet inside the drawer beneath, where my mother kept my father's slippers warm. I remember the smell of felt and wool mixed with the smell of my father's feet. It wasn't a bad smell. It was the smell of a father who loved me, who'd made a chair for me and who nursed me when I was sick. He nursed me throughout my childhood.

My mother had a hard time doing it because she always believed that I was faking it. She believed it because she had gone through her own childhood at the orphanage pretending to be sick, so that she could spend as much time as possible at the infirmary. The food there was better, the nurses were motherly, and in winter, it was warm. It took me years to understand why my mother wasn't at my side when I hurt, and more years still to stop feeling guilty when I was sick.

You always doubted me when I was sick!

There you go. As they said...

The apple...

Quite. I remember something else involving the little chair. One afternoon, the kitchen door had been left wide open, and I could see the entrance landing that seemed suspended in mid-air as it abruptly dropped into the spiral staircase that led downstairs. High above, daylight pierced through the Plexiglas panels that formed the ceiling of the auto-shop. I could hear my mother's voice coming from the apartment next door. I stood up grabbing my chair with both hands and holding it against my butt as I toddled out of the kitchen to the landing and then to the left through the open doorway of the other apartment. There, I put the chair down and sat.

In front of me was a narrow kitchen with another huge stove to the right, and on the far wall an enormous door that stood ajar. Beyond was a darker room, and that's where my mother's voice was coming from. I stood up once more, and holding the chair behind me, I quietly walked across the checkered linoleum floor to the doorway.

The next room was so dark it took me a while to adjust and see the old woman lying on a very high bed, her back propped against a couple of big pillows. She had a lace cap on her head and one crooked hand on her lap, with more lace at the wrist.

My mother was sitting on the side of the bed, holding the old woman's other crooked hand and cutting her nails. I could hear the *clip clip clip* sound the little scissors made. A weak yellow light came down from the ceiling, illuminating my mother's dark hair. There was a smell of urine in the air, and of something else I didn't recognize. Old age, probably. I remember standing there, holding the chair against my butt, staring at the scene.

I sat down again and I remember nothing else, except a feeling of satisfaction. I had come a long way after all, across a landing, an entire kitchen, and three doorways.

I like the clip clip clip sound, and the smell of old age. Reminds me of Mamie. Mamie's smell.

Dylan!

True, too!

I wouldn't call it a smell. More like a...

It was a smell, Mom.

A faint one then. A whiff. The flesh, I suppose. The flesh that ages and pulls away from the bones. In any case, Mamie doesn't wear a lace cap in bed.

That would be creepy.

Creepy?

The only lace cap I remember is the one in the Red Riding Hood story. The wolf is in bed instead of Granny; he has Granny in his stomach, and he is wearing a freaking lace cap on his head.

I remember. We didn't go beyond "Grandma, how big your ears are!" because at that point you slammed the book shut, insisting that it was a stupid story for stupid girls, and that that particular girl was particularly stupid since she didn't recognize a wolf when she saw one.

I said it like that?

No, of course not. You were so young, but that's what you meant.

See? I was already clever!

That, you were. Too clever for you own good.

FOURTEEN

"We have to reckon with the possibility that the psyche is not entirely confined to space and time." — Carl Jung

Dylan?

What?

Let's leave the present and the past, shall we? We've been there long enough, and we'll be taking them both with us anyway.

Where?

Into the future. Into the future to tie it all up, into the future or we'll remain here in limbo. Not a pleasant place to be. A bit like the purgatory of the believer. Neither here nor there. Trapped inside a misunderstanding, a question mark, an unfinished sentence. Better to follow the quote of the fictitious scriptures the way it was meant to be understood. "So let it be written, so let it be done."

You are going to write what shall be done.

Exactly.

***

Chicago, The Art Institute, July 2039

Adrian Hunter, his wife Mina, their teenage son Josh, and their twenty-two-year-old daughter Ariana are in town to see the most comprehensive exhibition ever shown of the history of Italian violinmaking. Ariana has insisted that they fly there from San Francisco since, after all, she will soon be a violinmaker herself.

After spending three years studying Italian and taking violin lessons at home, she is now a student at the prestigious *Scuola Internazionale di Liuteria* in Cremona, Italy. She will begin her fourth and final year there in September, and devote it entirely to the making of her own violin.

She has come to Chicago because the exhibit, conceived, gathered and organized in Milan by a young Italian curator, will be shown only in Italy after touring the Americas and the capitals of Europe.

"How can that be?" her mother asks. Mina has Italian blood, and anything about Italy is of great concern to her.

"Finances, Mama, always finances. The Americans probably paid an irresistible price and who can blame the museum in Milan. They're always in financial panic mode! The cost of maintaining the palazzo housing it, the cost of keeping the art safe, clean and protected, the cost of this, the cost of that. I should know; I spent my internship working at the Brera, and what the staff was mostly yapping about was money, money, money or rather the lack of it."

The time line of the exhibition begins in the mid-1500s with the creation of the first viola by Andrea Amati, and continues with the making of violins and other stringed instruments by his son, his grandson and their apprentices, some of whom, including Stradivari, became master crafters themselves. What is unique to this event, though, is that private collectors from around the world have lent their own treasures.

Among the most valued are paintings of the masters at work that have never been seen before, and correspondence spanning two hundred years between the luthiers and their clients, all wealthy amateurs, patrons and members of the royal courts of France, Spain and England.

Three large rooms are allocated to the exhibit. The first one has been designed to look like an atelier, one the Amati family might have built for themselves. Sunlight pours in from clerestory windows, the walls are lined with shelves loaded with instruments in all stages of construction. Trays of tools are neatly laid out on a large worktable standing in the center of the room.

Art students are playing the parts of apprentices, and you can see four youths in action as they gouge, carve, glue, and polish the wood. Another plays the old master, and goes from one youth to the other, correcting this and that, advising quietly.

Stimulated by the theatrics and activity, Josh has to be restrained from trying to touch everything.

"Stop acting like a five-year-old!" Ariana whispers angrily.

In the second room, the walls are covered with large screens on which play video loops of historical drawings and maps of Cremona and of Lombardy throughout the centuries. The walls of the last room are lined with paintings of the old masters in their workshops.

At the center of both the second and third rooms are long wooden glass-topped display cases featuring artifacts: original tools, parchments, letters and bills of sale, sketches of instruments at all stages of fabrication.

The cases in the third room are taller and contain original violins and bows.

Josh keeps whining like a five-year-old, "How boring!" and "Who cares about this stuff!" and "Let's go, Mama, please?" and finally, "Can't I wait in the cafeteria?"

"Shut up and learn something!" Ariana hisses back, and to her father, "I told you he should have stayed home! What a waste!"

Soon enough, Josh wins the fight and leaves for the cafeteria with a few dollars in his pocket and a winning smile on his face.

"He reminds me of my brother!" Adrian mutters.

That's when Ariana enters the last room. She begins touring the paintings, taking her time, enjoying each and every one of them. Until the fifth one that is, in front of which she freezes, transfixed by what she sees. According to the notation posted underneath, the painting depicts Nicoló Amati in his *bottega*, holding a violin in his right hand and looking down at three youths seated at a worktable.

Two of them are in profile as they look up at the master, while the third one stares at — what? At the viewer? If it was a photograph, he would be looking straight into the camera. That gives the painting an odd but compelling feeling of modernity. The young man is handsome, perhaps sixteen years old, but who can tell? He has a crown of thick, dark, wavy hair, eyes the color of dark chocolate that seem to eat up his entire face, and a sweet smirk on his lips. He is wearing a reddish shirt, open at the neck with its sleeves rolled up to his elbows. The painting is dated October 1650, and the painter is Henry Greensbury.

"Dad!" Ariana manages to call out without taking her eyes off the young man's face.

A few heads turn to look at her, and as if sensing a change in the air she pulls herself away from the painting, looks around and spots her father a few feet away in front of the central unit. She goes to him, grabs his arm and without a word leads him back to the fifth painting.

"There," she says haltingly.

Her father stares and says, "Jesus!"

"No, not Jesus," Ariana manages to answer. "Definitely not Jesus."

Mina, who has now caught up with them, shakes her head, unbelieving.

"Let's find the curator," decides Ariana. "We need to know more."

"Ari!" her father calls, pulling her back. "Wait. It's just a painting, sweetie. I know it's uncanny how like Dylan it looks, but every one of us has a lookalike somewhere in the world, right? We just found his, in the past. What else could it be?"

"Ancestry?"

"Impossible. I know where all my ancestors come from, and there is no one from Italy."

"That you know of. What about your grandmother? She was an orphan, wasn't she?"

"Yes, but physically Dylan took after my dad's side of

the family. All Russian Jews."

"As a young man, yes, but as a child he took after your French grandfather, didn't he?"

"He did, but my French grandfather's origins are settled. All French. All from the same small provincial town. We have the family tree to prove it, going back to the early 1600s. Nothing remotely Italian there."

"Maybe some Italians came over in the 1600s."

"Ari! Stop this nonsense. You are smarter than that."

But Ariana doesn't want to hear any of it. She shakes her father's hand off her arm and stomps out, repeating, "I'm going to find the curator."

Adrian takes off after her, sighing. "She is so like my mother, it's frightening."

"I'll be in the cafeteria with Josh," Mina calls out.

Arianna asks one of the docents to please call the curator, "We need to see her urgently."

"Something's wrong, miss?" the docent asks, worried by the agitation on Ariana's face.

"No, nothing's wrong. But we must see her."

"Give me a minute," replies the docent, moving aside and pulling out a phone from her breast pocket.

She speaks a while, then returns to explain that Miss Venturi is not presently at the institute, but that "her assistant is on his way down to see you."

A moment later a tall and painfully thin young man appears, announcing, "I am Frederico Antonelli, Miss Venturi's assistant. How can I be of assistance?"

He has a strong Italian accent, but his English is excellent.

"Come with us, please," Ariana tells him, and without explaining further she walks back to the third room and the fifth painting.

"How can we find out more about this painting?" she asks.

"I believe the sign here states pretty much all we know."

"The three youths," Ariana insists, "we'd like to know more about them. Their names, their..."

"I am not sure it's possible. Why are you so interested?"

Arianna asks her father to please show Mr. Antonelli a picture of Dylan.

Her father pulls out his phone and searches for a picture. He finds one of his brother as a teen.

"This one is striking," he says, showing it to Frederico.

Frederico looks at it, then looks up at the painting, then again at the picture before exclaiming softly, "How extraordinary!"

"We think so, too," Ariana says. "Have you ever seen such resemblance between a historical portrait and a modern youth?"

"Well, yes, when from the same family. Are you saying that this young man... what's his name — Dylan you said?"

"Yes, Dylan. Actually, his full name was Dylan-David. He was my brother," Adrian explains.

"He died many years ago," Ariana says, before adding unnecessarily, "He was twenty-three years old."

"Oh! I... I am sorry."

"Can we find out more about this painting, please?" she pleads.

"Well, I...let me think a minute. We do have a listing

of the students who trained at the Amatis' — of those who made it on their own that is, and entered into the registry of..." He shakes his head and then, as if coming to a decision he says firmly, "Come with me to the office. We will look in our database."

"Thank you!" Ariana says, flashing him a radiant smile.

"I'll text Mom," her father says. "She'll have to take Josh back to the hotel."

Three floors above the exhibit, they enter two connecting offices lent out to the staff traveling with the exhibition: the curator, Elena Venturi, her assistant Frederico Antonelli, and two art specialists with name tags hanging around their necks — Carla and Gianna, who are now busy preparing their move to the next venue.

Frederico goes straight to the screen that covers an entire side wall and enters a code in his phone before typing in "Nicolò Amati's students."

Thirteen names appear, each followed by the dates of their apprenticeship.

Pointing her finger, Ariana goes slowly down the list until she comes to the seventh name. There she stops, announcing, "Here he is: David Cacciatore, 1647 – 1652."

"How would you know?" Adrian asks.

Frederico exclaims, "Cacciatore! He was one of the first Baroque bow craftsmen to be known. Before him they were all anonymous. He shaped and carved his heads and frogs in such way that they became his signature. We have one of his bows downstairs in exhibit, lent by...

Everyone is talking at the same time. When they all

pause at once, Ariana tells her father, "Cacciatore, Daddy, means Hunter in Italian. David Cacciatore — Dylan-David Hunter minus Dylan. How about that?" She turns to Frederico. "What did you just say about bows and frogs?"

They search for more information but don't find much. No mention of David Cacciatore's date or place of birth, no mention of his life after the five years he spent studying with Nicolò Amati. Where did he go? What did he do? And how, Ariana wants to know, did Henry Greensbury, a British artist by the sound of it, come to paint in Cremona?

Frederico brings Henry Greensbury, baroque painter, on to the screen. They learn that he was, like his father before him, a British portraitist. A minor one, but nevertheless prolific, as he traveled back and forth between England and Italy on commission.

"Can you find out who his patrons were? His benefactors? Is there any work of his left, aside from this one, and if so, where? Also, was there any connection between the painter and the Cacciatore family?"

"Ari, slow down for heaven's sake!" her father says.

"Sorry," Ariana mumbles, looking at the screen which is now displaying Henry Greensbury's life.

Born in 1627, London, England, died in 1679, London.

Son of James Greensbury, portraitist to the court of King George II.

Studied under Flemish master Antoon van Dyck.

Moved to the city of Lodi, Italy, in the mid-1600s.

While there, he made several paintings of the Amati family in Cremona. He returned to London in 1669. What is left of his work resides in private collections in both England and Milan, Italy.

"Who lent you that particular painting?" Ariana asks Frederico.

"A private collector in London."

They keep reading.

Among his famous patrons were The Ergoton-Richmond, the Coutts, and — *here!* Ariana and Frederico exclaim as one — the Cacciatore family!

"Let's focus on the Cacciatores then," Frederico suggests as he brings name and period to the screen.

Guilio Cacciatore was born in 1622 in London, the son of a Milanese banker. He belonged to the group of moneylenders who modernized banking in England throughout the seventeenth century. His specialties were international trade and manufacturing. His son took over the direction of the bank at his father's death in 1687.

That, I am afraid, is it," Frederico says. "No mention anywhere of another son."

"How about a wife?"

"Nothing there, either."

"Damn."

Adrian looks at his phone, and tells Ariana, "A text from Mom. Time to go. We've been here a couple of hours, and I am sure Mr. Antonelli has more pressing things to do."

That's when Carla, one of the two art specialists who has been following their research from afar, calls, *Scusami?*

They all turn to her.

After explaining in broken English that she understands the language but cannot speak it, she addresses herself to Frederico in Italian.

When she is done, Ariana, exclaims, "What a brilliant

idea! Grazie mille, Carla." and to Frederico she asks, "Could we?"

"Of course," he says. "I am becoming as intrigued as you are."

Arianna explains to her father that when Carla doesn't travel with exhibitions around the world, she is on staff at the Museo della Musica in Lodi, and has, therefore, access to their archives online. "She suggests we look to see if Greensbury and David Cacciatore are anywhere mentioned."

"That sounds good," her father says. "But I'll have to leave you to it. Call when you are done."

"Thanks!" she says, hugging him.

"I wish I could stay, Ari, but Josh and Mom ..."

"I understand. Go, Dad, go."

Meanwhile, standing by the screen, Carla brings the Lodi files up to view.

Much later, at Chez Pierre restaurant

"So? Mina asks as soon as Ariana is seated. "Did you find out anything?"

"I am starving," her daughter replies, her face still flushed from her hurried journey through town.

"I am starving, too," Josh complains, lifting his head up from the game on his phone. "We've been waiting — like, forever!"

"Let's order then," their father says, signaling the waiter.

They order their food, then Ariana begins by saying, "It's both totally fascinating and impossible to know what to make of it."

"Just tell us!" her father says.

Arianna opens her notebook, explaining, "I took as many notes as I could so I wouldn't forget the essentials. It's a rather crowded tale!

"To begin with, Greensbury did indeed reside in Lodi from 1647 through 1651 and made a name, though minor, for himself by painting members of the Lombardy nobility. A few of his paintings are kept at the museum. What's more to our interest, though, is that he stayed the entire time at the villa of the Sforza family, the local gentry. We even have the address. It's located on the left bank of the river Adda. On its grounds today stands the town's main hospital. We can safely assume that Cosimo Sforza was an art lover and one of Greensbury's patrons. But who cares, right? What, on the other hand, we care very much about is that Clotilda Sforza, wife of Cosimo, was a Cacciatore!"

"Was she, now?" her father muses.

"She was from Milan so we can assume she was related to Guilio. A sister or a cousin maybe?"

"Any mention of Dylan? I mean, David?"

"I am getting there. Digging further, we found that Guilio's wife, a certain Andréa, visited Lodi at the time of Greensbury's presence. She too resided at the Sforzas' and bought a mandolin from the Amati family. Its bill of sale is still in the Sforzas' estate papers. Another compelling bill of sale is that of a commission for a painting by Greensbury of Nicolò Amati at work. That would be the one we saw at the museum. Signor Sforza paid the bill, but with the clear specification that the painting be sent to Andréa Cacciatore in London. It's coming together, isn't it?"

"Indeed. But what about David?"

"Nothing, and how odd! I mean, think about it. Andréa Cacciatore commissions a painting where David is obviously the centerpiece of the work rather than Nicolò Amati. Frederico and Carla both agree to that. The painter obviously instructed David to look straight at him. We can, therefore, assume that he is very dear to Andréa, and certainly from her family, since they share a last name. Was he her son?"

Their dinner over, they spend an hour or so strolling the streets of Chicago before returning to their hotel. At eleven thirty p.m. Ariana and her brother enter their room while their parents go to the bar for a last drink.

Josh stretches himself on his bed, puts on his headphones and clicks on the wall screen in search of entertainment.

Arianna is busy re-reading her notes when she gets a long mail from Carla. She reads it, and then she reads it again before rushing out of the room and down to the bar.

"Guess what?" she asks her parents.

"What?"

"Just got a message from Carla. She's found David."

"She has? How? Where?"

"In France!"

"In France?"

"Yes, in Paris! She kept thinking about the mystery of him when she realized that there was another way, a better way to learn what had become of him. She went back to her files and the private collector who had lent them David's bow for the exhibition. From there she researched its historical journey. That took her from London to Edinburgh and finally to Paris, where in 1659, seven years after the end of his apprenticeship in Cremona, David Cacciatore opened a luthier shop on the Faubourg Saint-Antoine. The location makes sense since that area of the city was then the center of craftsmanship.

"The workshop, called *Cinque*, was listed in the tightly regulated French Guild of Craftsmen, under the sub-group of *Maîtres Luthiers*. Carla, like all professional specialists of art history, has access to all the European files on arts and crafts guilds now regrouped in a single archive.

"David sold Amati violins, meaning that he was now probably a sort of dealer for his old master. He also sold bows of his own making.

"In 1665, Sir James Delmey Raphline, a young British aristocrat, bought the very bow that's now on exhibit, and an Amati violin in David's workshop. Upon his death in 1718, both violin and bow were given to a private museum in Edinburg. By the mid-1800s, the bow was back in London, in private hands."

"What an extraordinary young man David Cacciatore must have been!" Mina muses. "When you think that the seventeenth century was an era of carriages and constant political instability that made traveling both taxing and dangerous, and that he, who was probably born in England if indeed he was Andréa's son, went all the way to Italy to study the art of violinmaking, and then back to Paris to open his own workshop. What a courageous life!"

"He might have been from the Milanese side of the

family," Adrian suggests. "That would explain his studying in Cremona."

"That doesn't feel right," Ariana retorts, frustrated. "Why would Andréa, who lives in England, travel so far just to visit her husband's nephew and have a very personal portrait made of him?"

"There is that. But why, then, isn't David mentioned as Guilio's son anywhere? Come to think of it, he isn't mentioned anywhere near any of the Cacciatores. Was he perhaps disowned? And if so, why? He was just a boy!"

"And why, if he was Andréa and Guilio's son, didn't he return to London? Why stop in Paris?"

"That's easy to answer," Ariana says. "The arts were in Paris. Paris was already where everything was happening!"

"Okay, then," Mina recapitulates. "Let's say he was around fifteen years old in Cremona in 1650. That puts him at age thirty in Paris in 1665. He certainly lived longer than your brother," she adds, looking at her husband. "Speaking of which, we still don't have a clue why there would be a clone-like resemblance."

"No, we don't," Ariana says, "and I don't think we ever will. Still. There has to be a connection there. I am so damn sure of it!"

"We'll have to ask your grandmother," her father says. "She no doubt has something to do with this!"

"Are you serious?" Mina laughs.

"Absolutely. My mother always insisted that had he lived in another time, a much older time, Dylan would have survived," Adrian says.

"That would be quite like her to have written him down into history!" Ariana adds wistfully.

Rolling his eyes, her father stands up and says, "Come on, you two, enough with the silliness. Let's go get some sleep!"

FIFTEEN

Dylan?

Yes?

It is done. I have told your story and given you a life well-lived.

You have. Einstein would be proud.

It doesn't make the reality of your absence any better, but it helps.

... ...

Dylan?

Yes?

Don't go, please. I couldn't bear it.

It's up to you. I am stuck in your head, remember?

In my heart, Dylan, in my heart.

You always said it's the same thing.

It is, but the heart is the part where emotions rule. I am not talking about the physical heart, the one that pumps the blood, but the other heart, the one you can't expose and pull apart to make a diagnosis.

Back to the head, then?

I suppose. It's where the intellect roams, it's where the spirit is, the psyche — the immaterial sum of all of us.

I still question its beginning, though, its expanse, its location. Could the brain only be a conduit?

Whatever, Mom. Have you forgiven me?

There was never anything to forgive, Dylan. Only plenty to understand and come to terms with. But as you know, as you experienced it so hopelessly yourself, understanding is always an elusive proposition.

Are you better healed now?

No. I am not healed at all, and never will be. It was never a matter of healing, only of living. Living for your father, living for your brother, living to remember you.

***

Mom?

Yes?

Whenever you want to pretend, don't forget. I'll be there.

Oakland, December 2018

ABOUT ATMOSPHERE PRESS

Atmosphere Press is an independent, full-service publisher for excellent books in all genres and for all audiences. Learn more about what we do at atmospherepress.com.

We encourage you to check out some of Atmosphere's latest releases, which are available at Amazon.com and via order from your local bookstore:

The Unordering of Days, poetry by Jessica Palmer

It's Not About You, poetry by Daniel Casey

Skinny Vanilla Crisis, a novel by Colleen Alles

The Mommy Clique, a novel by Barbara Altamirano

Pandemic Aftermath: How Coronavirus Changed Global Society, nonfiction by Trond Undheim

A Dream of Wide Water, poetry by Sharon Whitehill

Radical Dances of the Ferocious Kind, poetry by Tina Tru

Odo and the Stranger, a picture book by Mark Johnson

The Woods Hold Us, poetry by Makani Speier-Brito

Olive, a novel by Barbara Braendlein

My Cemetery Friends: A Garden of Encounters at Mount Saint Mary in Queens, New York, nonfiction and poetry by Vincent J. Tomeo

Change in 4D, nonfiction by Wendy Wickham

Disruption Games: How to Thrive on Serial Failure, nonfiction by Trond Undheim

Itsuki, a novel by Zach MacDonald

A Surprising Measure of Subliminal Sadness, short stories by Sue Powers

ABOUT THE AUTHOR

Dominique Hunter was born and raised in the Languedoc, a region in the south of France. In 1979, she moved to Berkeley, California. She married an American and had two sons. She loves animals, American Jazz and the cello. She resides in Oakland with her husband and Babette, her sassy Aussie.

CPSIA information can be obtained
at www.ICGtesting.com
Printed in the USA
FSHW011824261020
75174FS